1811.

STILL IN STEAM

Still in Steam

G. M. KICHENSIDE
and R. C. RILEY

LONDON
IAN ALLAN

First published 1969

SBN 7110 0106 5

Published by Ian Allan Ltd, Shepperton, Surrey and printed in the United Kingdom by Morrison & Gibb Ltd., London and Edinburgh

641 BXXX 869

Contents

COVER PHOTOGRAPH: Keighley & Worth Valley
Railway Ivatt 2–6–2T No 41241 heads a train from
Keighley to Oxenhope over Mytholmes viaduct on
August 3, 1968.   [Derek Cross

1 *A thumbnail history of railways in Britain*

NOBODY really knows when the first railway was built. They were first described in the 16th century, but these " rail " ways were nothing like those to which we are accustomed today. The rails were of timber and merely formed guideways for small wagons used in connection with primitive industries of the time. The wagons would have been pushed by men or hauled by horses; the lines were no more than a few hundred yards long and were used to convey material from a mine or quarry. As coal mining and iron ore working became established industries, and with the beginning of the industrial revolution in the 18th and 19th centuries, industrial wagonways and tramroads became more widespread. Indeed, by 1801 thoughts were turned towards the use of railways to carry goods and even passengers from one town to another.

The Surrey Iron Railway was opened in 1804 for the carriage of goods from Wandsworth, where it had river access, to Croydon. The first railway to carry passengers was that between Swansea and Oystermouth opened in 1806 but both this and the Surrey Iron Railway employed horses to pull the wagons and passenger vehicles. It was not until the development of the steam locomotive that railways became a more suitable means of carrying goods and people over longer distances.

In the late 1700s and early 1800s a number of pioneer inventors had tried building self-propelled steam engines, mostly for use on roads but one or two for railways. Few were really successful. By 1815 George Stephenson, who was employed at Killingworth Colliery in Northumberland, had improved on the pioneer designs and produced a railway steam locomotive known as the Killingworth type which was used later on a number of colliery lines. In 1825 a new railway was opened between Stockton and Darlington, followed in 1830

by railways between Liverpool and Manchester, and Canterbury and Whitstable. A development of the Killingworth locomotive was built for the Stockton & Darlington by the newly-formed locomotive building works of Robert Stephenson, George Stephenson's son, the now famous *Locomotion No. 1*, still preserved today at Darlington. The Stockton & Darlington Railway was in fact the first in the World to use steam locomotives, although they were employed only for goods trains, and the passenger trains were still hauled by horses, The Liverpool & Manchester Railway, in contrast. planned to use steam locomotives for all traffic; in order to find the most reliable and economic types a series of trials was organised at Rainhill in 1829. The most successful locomotive to be entered was *The Rocket*, built by the Stephensons; this locomotive is preserved at the Science Museum in London.

From these early beginnings commercial railways became a practical possibility. The following decade saw the opening of numerous lines, including the first long-distance routes between London and Birmingham, London and Bristol, and London and Southampton. At the same time numerous local lines sprang up in many parts of the country, at first completely isolated but soon linked with one another by end-on connections or junctions and spurs. George and Robert Stephenson surveyed many of the routes and, indeed, were appointed engineers in charge of construction.

One problem soon to emerge was the question of gauge. George Stephenson set the pattern for railway gauges in Great Britain when he adopted 4ft 8½in between the inside edge of the rails. This was the gauge with which he was familiar on the colliery railways in Northumberland. Its origin is obscure but one explanation is that the wagon wheels of the time were 5ft wide over their outside faces; allowing for the thickness of a wheel 4ft 8½in was the approximate measurement between the inside edges, which was where the flange was placed to guide the wheel on a rail. Thus all the

LEFT: Winter on the KWVR; the line's North Eastern Class J72 0–6–0T *Joem* leaves Haworth for Oxenhope with the 1pm train from Keighley on February 2, 1969.
[J. B. Mounsey

IT ALL STARTED HERE

LEFT: Most famous of the pioneer locomotives is Stephenson's *Rocket*, built for the Liverpool & Manchester Rainhill trials in 1829. The original survives in the Science Museum in London but a replica also exists and is seen in this photograph.　　[British Railways

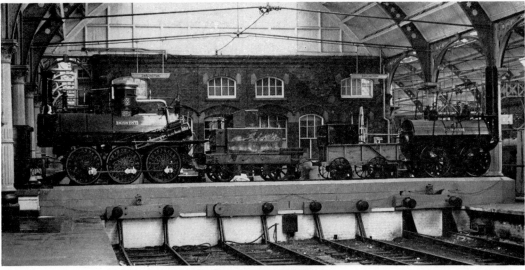

ABOVE: Two other pioneer locomotives have been preserved, 0–6–0 *Derwent* and 0–4–0 *Locomotion* of the Stockton & Darlington Railway. They are displayed on the concourse at Darlington station.
[British Railways

LEFT: Another early locomotive still in existence is the Liverpool & Manchester 0–4–2 *Lion*, which remains in working order. It has frequently been used for filming and was the star character in *The Titfield Thunderbolt*.　　[British Railways

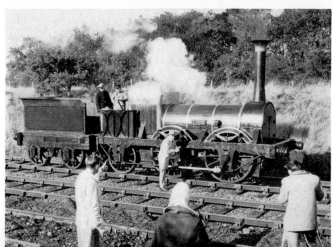

railways with which the Stephensons were connected were built to this gauge.

Other engineers, particularly Isambard Kingdom Brunel, who surveyed and engineered the Great Western Railway, decided that higher speeds and better riding could be given by a wider track and adopted a gauge of 7ft 0¼in for the railway between London and Bristol. In the following years as new railways were built the broad gauge extended into parts of the West Midlands and from Bristol to Plymouth. With broad-gauge track also employed on lines in Cornwall a through broad-gauge route was ultimately established between London and Penzance. It was soon realised, however, by Parliament that chaos would ensue if different railways adopted individual gauges. By 1846 a commission, established to examine the gauge question, reported in favour of 4ft 8½in gauge and the Great Western and its allies with broad gauge lines were forced to abandon the broad gauge over a period of years. Although the GWR had used standard gauge for certain of its lines from the 1840s by the expedient of laying mixed gauge track, and started to convert its broad gauge lines to standard gauge in the late 1860s, broad gauge did not finally disappear until 1892 when the last sections of line not already equipped for mixed gauge running were converted to standard gauge in one weekend.

Meanwhile during the 1840s and 1850s new railways blossomed in their hundreds. Many were merely proposed and never saw the light of day and many were competing schemes for lines already in existence. It must be remembered that railways were the fastest means of transport in the world and were the obvious things in which to invest capital. Until the coming of the railway the fastest means of transport had been the horse, with maximum speeds for short sprints of up to 30mph but more often averaging 10–15mph with the mail and stage coaches of the pre-railway age. Almost overnight speeds of 40, 50, or even 60mph were being achieved with steam locomotives.

Gradually local lines joined forces with each other, for it was clearly more economic to have a common administration supervising a through route. Thus in 1844 the Midland Railway was formed by an amalgamation of a number of companies in the Midlands area between Leicester and York, while two years later the London & North Western Railway came into existence with the amalgamation of the London & Birmingham and Grand Junction railways. Yet even more local lines were built, now often feeders from towns not on a through route to a junction with a main line. Totnes to Ashburton for example was opened in 1872, and Keighley to Oxenhope in 1867.

By the 1890s the railway map would be very familiar to us today but some important lines had still to be built; the London extension of the Manchester, Sheffield & Lincolnshire Railway from Nottingham through Leicester and Rugby to Marylebone was not opened until 1899, while the direct routes from Paddington to Birmingham via Bicester and Paddington to South Wales via Badminton were not opened until the first years of the present century. With the exception of a few suburban lines and particularly underground railways in London, by 1910 the British railway map was complete. Indeed, it reached its peak at this time for, by 1900, another contender for public transport had appeared on the scene, the internal combustion engine, which threatened the railways' monopoly. A third challenger was the electric motor which was quickly adopted by towns and cities for powering trams running on street railways, which until then had still been powered by horses.

It was the electric tram which soon began to challenge steam-operated railways for suburban traffic in the larger towns. The railways themselves looked towards more economical methods of operation in an endeavour to counter the opposition. Some adopted a new type of unit, a rail motor, that is a passenger coach propelled by a self-contained steam engine mounted at one end of the carriage body. The disadvantage of this type of unit was that it was unable to carry an unexpected increase in passengers on special occasions. From the steam railcar came the push-pull train used on some branches and main line local services. This type of train consisted of from one to four coaches coupled to a generally small tank engine. The coach furthest from the locomotive was equipped with a driver's cab and controls linked to the regulator on the engine and for braking. The engine pulled the train in one direction but pushed it in the other with the driver riding on the leading coach. The push-pull train did not need run-round facilities at terminal stations and track layouts on some branches were simplified for this type of working.

In 1903 the railways themselves ventured into electric traction when suburban lines in Newcastle and Liverpool were electrified. By the outbreak of the first world war in 1914 a number of London suburban lines had been electrified, including the beginnings of what later became the great Southern electric system. But these measures could not be

This group of four photographs shows typical express trains at the turn of the century; representatives of all the locomotive classes seen here have been preserved.

ABOVE: Midland 4–2–2 No 683 with a down express near Mill Hill.

[Locomotive Publishing Co

justified where traffic was low and during the first world war passenger services were withdrawn from a few routes where it was no longer possible to maintain an economic service. Apart from early closures in the mid- and late-19th century of lines which had failed in their quest and which should never have been built in the first place, these were the first closures of uneconomic lines so familiar today.

At this time it was also realised that the many railway companies then in existence competing with each other for traffic was doing nobody any good. Although many smaller lines had amalgamated or been taken over to form larger concerns, there were still more than 120 railway companies in existence; not all owned any locomotives and coaches which were provided by neighbouring companies. There were also numerous joint lines owned by two or more partners; some such as the Midland & Great Northern and Somerset & Dorset were important cross-country routes with their own engines and rolling stock. In others the joint partners owned the track and stations etc. but the trains belonged to the individual partners and not to the joint concern.

In 1921 Parliament passed an Act which grouped practically all the many railway companies into four big groups, the London Midland & Scottish, the London & North Eastern, the Great Western and the Southern. New administrations were set

BELOW: GN Stirling 4–2–2 No 1003 heads a down semi-fast train near Hitchin in the years before the first world war.

[W. J. Reynolds

ABOVE: SE&C Class D 4–4–0 No 505 heads an up Dover-London boat train through the Warren near Folkestone in about 1910. [Locomotive Publishing Co

up for each of the new companies, and standardised locomotives, stock, other equipment and, in particular, liveries were evolved. The passing of the varied colour schemes of the smaller railways was mourned by enthusiasts of the time and certainly, with few exceptions, we have not seen such colourful engine and carriage liveries since then, although fortunately many survive on locomotives which have subsequently been preserved. Although competition was much reduced it still survived on certain routes, for example between London and Scotland (LMS and LNER), between London and the Midlands (LMS and GWR) and to the west of England (GWR and SR). Indeed, there were still three major routes from London to

Scotland, three to Sheffield, and two to Leeds, Manchester, Liverpool, Birmingham, Exeter and Plymouth.

But with the exception of suburban services in certain provincial towns railway services carried on much as before. Steam traction was still supreme and although a few line closures occurred in the 1920s and 1930s most services continued. New types of express steam locomotives were being developed, particularly the Coronation Class Pacifics on the LMS and the streamlined Class A4 Pacifics on the LNER, one of which, *Mallard*, achieved the world's speed record for steam traction in 1938 with a maximum of 126mph. This engine has since been preserved and may be seen in

BELOW: GWR Dean Atbara class 4–4–0 No 3395 *Aden* heads a down train from Paddington, composed entirely of clerestory roof coaches, at Goring troughs in 1905.

ABOVE: What is generally accepted to be the first railway enthusiasts' special excursion took place in 1938 when GNR Stirling 4–2–2 No 1 was brought out of York Museum for a number of special runs, in company with some old ECJS and GNR six-wheeled coaches.

Clapham Museum. But in the south of England with the relatively short runs between London and the South Coast, where fast and frequent services were needed, electrification was employed. The Southern Railway not only extended its suburban electric network in the 1920s and 1930s but between 1932 and 1938 converted the main lines to Brighton, Hastings, Bognor and Portsmouth.

Nevertheless, during the period between the first and second world wars economic factors seriously influenced railway operation; one of the earlier competitors, the internal combustion engine, now made serious inroads into rail transport, for not only had petrol-engined buses been developed for city use they had also been introduced on many country routes and were thus in direct competition with branch line and cross-country railway services. Moreover, private cars were increasing.

Although as mentioned earlier a standard gauge of 4ft 8½in was evolved for railways in Great Britain it did not mean that other gauges were not used. Indeed, narrow gauge lines with rails only 3ft apart or even less were used on numerous lines. All were, however, local in character and often connected with industry. The reason for the use of narrow gauge lines was economy since such lines could be built very much more cheaply than those of standard gauge. The track bed was much narrower, sleepers were shorter, rails were of lighter section and locomotives and rolling stock smaller and lighter. Moreover, curves could be much sharper and gradients more severe than could be tolerated on main lines. As we also mentioned, some of the earliest railways were merely wagon-

ways for serving the newly-developing coal and iron industries; in Wales, narrow gauge lines were built to bring slate from the mountains in the west and north to the coastal ports. Among them were the Talyllyn and Festiniog railways. Horses were used to haul the wagons; on the Festiniog, horses hauled the empty wagons uphill from the port to the quarry face but the loaded trains ran downhill by gravity in the charge of a brakesman, the horse riding on a special truck.

By the 1860s, however, steam traction had been adopted on narrow gauge lines and a few of the pioneer locomotives on the Welsh narrow gauge lines survive in working order to this day.

While some of these industrial railways carried passengers, other narrow gauge lines were built primarily for passengers to link towns with nearby main lines. Passenger services on narrow gauge railways in Great Britain however, were among the earliest to be hit by road competition, particularly in the 1920s and 1930s. Among those closed during this period were the Southwold Railway in Suffolk, the Lynton & Barnstaple in Devon, the Leek & Manifold Valley in Staffordshire and the Campbeltown & Macrihanish in West Scotland. Others, like the Welshpool & Llanfair, had their passenger services withdrawn but remained open for freight. Both the Festiniog and Talyllyn Railways and one or two others in Wales struggled on through the second world war, although in very run down condition with an irregular service of passenger and freight trains and, soon after the second world war, as we shall see later, the Festiniog closed down and became derelict.

2 Closures and modernisation on British Railways

THE MAIN LINES, too, did not escape for during the 1930s the LMS closed a number of intermediate stations on main lines and a few more branches were axed. But it was not until the end of the second world war and after nationalisation in 1948 that the plight of the railways became serious. Rail services had hardly been profitable between the wars, now many were running at a loss. As road competition from both buses and private cars gradually took passengers away from country railway routes closures followed. The railways themselves introduced new freight operating methods whereby the small amounts of freight normally carried by branch lines were handled by road to and from major railheads in industrial centres.

There was clearly little future for the majority of branch lines. On main lines, too, country stations with sparse traffic were closed and alternative buses provided instead to link with trains at larger towns some miles away. The closure programme was accelerated by the Beeching Plan evolved in 1963 which foreshadowed the closure of the majority of branch and intermediate local stations. In the view of Dr. Beeching the railway's main function was to carry passengers or freight at high speeds between large centres of population, leaving road transport to cater for smaller towns and villages.

A few years before this in 1955 British Railways had embarked on a vast modernisation plan which envisaged the complete changeover from steam locomotives to diesel traction and electrification. Within only two or three years diesel locomotives began to appear and diesel multiple-units, self-powered passenger trains with diesel engines mounted under the carriage floor, gradually took over many local and branch services. The multiple-unit is a flexible form of train since it is a self-contained unit with its own power, and driving cabs at each end. Normally they are made up of two, three or four-coach formations, but if a train has to be lengthened to cope with additional traffic two or more units can be coupled together and driven from the leading cab by one man. The through control cables allow him to work all the engines simultaneously from his control desk. Many electric trains are similarly formed into multiple-units; in this case, however, power is provided by electric traction motors fed from a live rail alongside the running rails or from overhead catenary.

Although diesel multiple-unit trains were introduced to many branch and cross-country services in an endeavour to cut operating costs, in many instances traffic was not sufficient to provide an economic diesel service and many have since been withdrawn. Other methods have been tried to cut operating costs, for example, the simplification of signalling and the conversion of stations to un-staffed halts, with tickets issued by a conductor guard on the train; even these measures in many instances have not proved successful.

With the closure programme proceeding more rapidly in the 1960s, except for the highly complex Southern electric network which, with further conversions, now covers most of Southern England from Bournemouth in the west to Dover in the east including the outer suburban areas around London, the important inter-city main lines now have few intermediate stations. On the Western Region main line between Paddington and Bristol instead of the former 15 or so stations in the 40-odd miles between Didcot and Bath there are now only two, at Swindon and Chippenham.

In 1968 we saw the culmination of the original 1955 modernisation plan, for British Railways withdrew its last steam locomotive. The main lines between Euston, Birmingham, Manchester and Liverpool have been electrified on the high voltage overhead system and so, too, have outer suburban lines from Liverpool Street in the Eastern Region and around Glasgow. Other than these routes and the Southern electric system, diesel locomotives or multiple-units operate all services. Since most main line stopping trains and branch services have disappeared BR concentrates primarily

ASHBURTON

During Easter 1969 the Dart Valley Light Railway Company reopened part of the former GWR Ashburton branch between Totnes and Buckfastleigh. The remaining section on to Ashburton is still under discussion as this book closed for press, since the Ministry of Transport plans to use part of the line for road improvements. ABOVE: A scene on the branch at Ashburton before passenger services were withdrawn; GW 0–4–2T No 1427 stands at Ashburton on July 2, 1957. BELOW: The same station in July 1964 after the line had been closed.

[R. C. Riley (2)

on the operation of inter-city passenger services and long-distance freight haulage.

Freight services themselves have been revolutionised. The slow clanking goods train of the past stopping to shunt wagons at intermediate stations and then being remarshalled two or three times on its journey has almost gone. Instead we have block trains, that is sets of wagons which are hardly ever uncoupled, running between important industrial centres conveying such materials as oil, coal, cement, steel products, car components, etc. For general freight we have the Freightliner, trains of long bogie flat wagons carrying containers, running at high speeds of up to 75mph. The containers are designed to be carried on road vehicles to give direct collection and delivery from manufacturer to user; the containers are also designed to be carried on ships to Europe and North America to provide through transport without the goods being unloaded until reaching their destination.

Thus the end of steam has also seen the end of the old type railway, familiar for so many years, and British Railways must clearly look to the future not to the past. However, that does not mean to say that we should forget the past for it is part of our history. Without steam locomotives and the early railways we should not have modern railways. There are many people in this country who like to see steam locomotives in action and some have grouped together to try and keep short sections of railway working exactly as they were in the steam era. We have already seen that economic factors were one of the reasons why the steam locomotive came to an end on British Railways. Each engine needed two men to operate it, coal was expensive and the engine needed servicing after almost every trip. Its performance too, depended on the ability of the fireman to keep the fire going to provide

HORSTED KEYNES

BELOW: Horsted Keynes station on the former LBSCR line between East Grinstead and Lewes, seen in 1953 with Ivatt Class 2 2–6–2T No 41297 heading a Lewes train. The line was later closed by British Railways but Horsted Keynes now forms the northern end of the Bluebell Railway.　　　　　[R. C. Riley

END OF AN ERA

August 11, 1968 will go down in history as the day on which British Railways ran its last steam train; this was a special excursion from Liverpool to Carlisle and was headed on the start of the journey from Liverpool to Manchester by Stanier Class 5 4–6–0 No 45110 (LEFT); from Manchester to Carlisle it was hauled by Britannia Pacific No 70013 *Oliver Cromwell*, seen at Ais Gill (BELOW) where a stop was made for photography. No 45110 has since been preserved by the Flairavia Flying Club of Biggin Hill, while No 70013 is preserved at Bressingham Hall near Diss.   [John H. Bird; I. S. Carr

START OF A NEW ERA

ABOVE: The beginning of the railway preservation movement in Great Britain in 1951; on May 14, 1951 the Talyllyn Railway Preservation Society reopened the Talyllyn line for passengers, and the first train is about to leave Towyn Wharf station. [P. B. Whitehouse

RIGHT: Locomotive preservation means sheer hard slogging to restore engines to a presentable condition, apart from any work necessary to keep the locomotive mechanically sound. Here members of the Class C Preservation Society are seen at work on their SE&C 0-6-0 No 592 at Ashford. [D. A. Idle

steam in sufficient quantity. In marked contrast is a modern electric locomotive controlled by one man who by the mere turn of a handle can produce speeds regularly and reliably of 100mph or more.

Thus the surviving steam railways cannot possibly run on a normal commercial basis and the people who run them do so for the most part voluntarily without pay. They operate the lines in their own time at weekends and during holidays, for at other times they have their normal work to perform elsewhere. Several of these railways are already operating train services and others are planned. They are privately-owned, since, as we have just seen, British Railways' function is to run a modern railway. For this purpose groups of enthusiasts have raised money or obtained financial backing to buy closed branch lines from British Railways and to acquire steam locomotives and coaches still in working order. It is not as simple as that, of course, since you cannot just buy a line and run a passenger service. In this country the

s.s.—2

Ministry of Transport keeps a close watch on railway operation whether it is run by British Railways or a private company. Before any sales of branch lines to a private organisation are approved the new owners must satisfy the Minister of Transport that they are capable of running a railway safely and in accordance with the strict operating rules. Although the privately-operated railways usually have a small permanent paid staff, volunteer enthusiasts help to run and maintain the line. Indeed, many of the volunteers are railwaymen themselves working their normal turns on British Railways and spending their off-duty time on a private railway. Some engine crews regretted the passing of the steam locomotive on BR and they find an outlet for their enthusiasm on the privately-owned steam locomotives. In later chapters we describe the lines still in steam and the many static museums and displays of relics organised by railway enthusiasts, municipal authorities and by British Railways itself.

3 Locomotives

WE HAVE already described how George Stephenson developed the Killingworth type colliery engine of the early 1800s into the successful locomotive which won the Rainhill trials in 1829 in readiness for the opening of the Liverpool & Manchester Railway. As new railways were built so more locomotives were required. Some had four wheels, others six, while some engines on the Great Western had eight wheels. Most had only a pair of driving wheels which were usually larger in diameter than the remaining carrying wheels. Steam locomotives are normally described by their wheel arrangement; the wheels are divided into groups depending on whether they are purely for carrying or guiding the locomotive or whether they are driving wheels actually forcing the locomotive along. The Great Western eight-wheel locomotives just mentioned were in fact 4–2–2s since they had four carrying wheels in front, two driving wheels, one on each side, and two more carrying wheels under the footplate. The *Rocket* in contrast had one pair of large driving wheels in the front and a pair of carrying wheels at the back and was thus an 0–2–2 since it did not have any guiding or carrying wheels in front of the driving wheels.

Gradually locomotives were built a little larger and were provided with additional carrying or driving wheels depending on the type. Passenger engines, for example, often had four driving wheels, two on each side, with a coupling rod linking the driving wheels on each side so that both pairs turned in unison. Thus a locomotive with two carrying wheels in front and four driving wheels is described as a 2–4–0. If the carrying wheels are at the back under the cab the engine is an 0–4–2. It was soon realised that engines for hauling goods trains needed most if not all their weight for adhesion, that is for the weight to bear on the driving wheels to reduce the risk of the wheels slipping when hauling a heavy train. Thus some engines were provided with six driving wheels and no carrying wheels, and were described as 0–6–0s. By the 1860s engines were beginning to look a little less like the *Rocket* and a little more like the locomotives

familiar to our own eyes since they had grown in length, boilers were larger, chimneys, now carried on top of the smokebox instead of emerging from the front, were shorter. Primitive cabs were provided to give the enginemen shelter against the wind and rain. Generally speaking engines for passenger traffic had two or four driving wheels and those for goods trains had six driving wheels. The engines with only two driving wheels were in fact often referred to as "singles" or "single drivers" since when seen from one side of the locomotive it appeared to have only one driving wheel. Sometimes the wheels of express passenger engines were very large, over 7ft in many cases, since locomotive designers thought that higher speeds could be obtained by having larger wheels. By the 1890s the 4–4–0 type had become standard for most express passenger trains but as trains became longer, and heavier coaches came into use, larger engines still were needed to cope with the heavier train weights.

The logical development of the 4–4–0 type was the 4–4–2, often called the "Atlantic" type, since engines of this wheel arrangement were first seen in America. Other designers thought that it would be better to increase the number of driving wheels and so the 4–6–0 type was developed at about the turn of the century. As train weights continued to increase with the introduction of corridor vehicles, dining cars, sleeping cars, etc. as we shall see later, even more powerful engines were required, culminating in the 4–6–2 design, the "Pacifics", the first of which was built by the Great Western Railway in 1908 and later from 1922 by the GNR and LNER, from 1933 by the LMS and from 1941 by the Southern Railway. These engines were built to the maximum size and weight permitted by the British loading gauge and were among the most powerful types produced in Great Britain. Indeed, one of the LNER Pacifics, No. 4468 *Mallard*, preserved at Clapham Museum, holds the world's speed record for steam traction of 126mph.

Until the turn of the century small 0–6–0s were the main types used on goods trains but as train lengths increased so too did the need for larger freight engines. Many of the designs produced since then had eight coupled wheels; in recent years British Railways introduced a ten coupled locomotive of the 2–10–0 wheel arrangement. To replace the miscellaneous assortment of 2–4–0s, 4–4–0s, etc. dating from the turn of the century or earlier, recent years saw the introduction of 2–6–0s and 4–6–0s, known as mixed traffic types, for general purpose duties, capable of working any type of train whether it be local or express passenger, slow freight trains or parcels trains.

So far we have spoken only of tender locomotives but from the early days a type of locomotive was developed which carried its coal and water supplies in tanks and bunkers mounted on the engine frame and not carried in a separate tender coupled to the locomotive. The water tanks were often alongside the boiler. In some cases they were slung in tanks carried on each side of the boiler, although not standing on the main frames (pannier tanks) or in a curved tank on top of the boiler (saddle tank). There were a few designs in which the tanks were placed between the frames under the boiler (well tanks). While many of the smaller tank engine designs were intended for shunting or local goods trains, some of the larger types were used on stopping passenger or short distance express workings. They were particularly useful for working local services into big city centres, since they did not need turning and could run equally well forwards or backwards.

Tank engines were built in all shapes and sizes ranging from the diminutive 0–6–0Ts of the London, Brighton & South Coast Railway and the South Eastern & Chatham Railway, used for light passenger duties, to 0–4–4Ts, 0–6–2Ts and 4–4–2Ts used by a number of lines for general short-distance passenger work. In more recent years 2–6–2Ts and 2–6–4Ts became established for local and branch workings. To replace the multiplicity of engine types inherited by British Railways in 1948 from the four group companies 12 standard classes were evolved—three 4–6–2s, two 4–6–0s, three 2–6–0s, a 2–6–4T, two types of 2–6–2T, and the 2–10–0 for heavy freight. As it turned out the British Railways standard classes by no means replaced the earlier types of steam locomotive, for the dieselisation and electrification programme, part of the 1955 modernisation plan, brought about the end of steam traction on British Railways in 1968 with several of the pre-nationalisation types, particularly the LMS Class 5 4–6–0s and Class 8 2–8–0s, surviving until the end.

Although steam locomotives no longer exist on BR lines they survive on the private railways and it is still a source of interest to the non-technical observer to know how a steam locomotive works. The steam locomotive has five main parts, the firebox, boiler, smokebox, cylinders and wheels. The firebox is situated at one end of the boiler and indeed forms part of it, since the firebox itself is within the boiler. Tubes from the firebox carry the smoke and gases from the burning coal through the boiler to the smokebox, where they are exhausted through the chimney. The fire in the firebox and the hot exhaust gases passing through the tubes heat the water in the boiler and turn it into steam, which accumulates in the top of the boiler at high pressure of between about 160lb and 250lb per sq in depending on the design of the locomotive. When the driver wants the locomotive to move, he opens the regulator handle controlling the regulator valve. Steam passes through the regulator valve, which is usually situated in the dome, and in most engines passes to the cylinders. Some locomotives, however, are fitted with superheaters in which the steam is led through more tubes inside the fire tubes. This has the effect of drying the steam and gives additional power; many of the earlier and smaller locomotives were not fitted with this refinement.

When the steam reaches the cylinders it is guided by the cylinder valves into one end or the other of the cylinder proper, where it expands, the force pushing a piston backwards and forwards as the steam is admitted first to one end and then the other. The piston is connected to the driving wheels and as it moves forwards and backwards so the connecting rod pulls and pushes the wheels round to make them turn and thus the locomotive moves. Other rods linked to the driving wheels cause the cylinder valves to move backwards and forwards which thus admit steam to the cylinders at just the right moment. When the steam has finished its work in the cylinder it passes out through the cylinder valves into the smokebox where it is ejected through the chimney with the firebox gases as a puff. The steam still has plenty of power left in for it helps to draw the exhaust gases from the firebox and thus maintains a draught to keep the fire burning brightly. As it is exhausted out of the chimney the smoke and steam provide spectacular effects when the engine is working hard.

Normally engines have two cylinders but some types have three or even four. The pistons are arranged so that each is in a different part of the cycle of events in the cylinders; thus at a given moment live steam is entering the cylinder from the

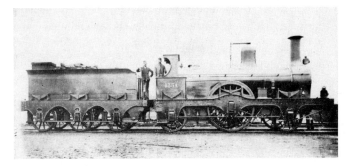

LOCOMOTIVE DEVELOPMENT 1860-1930

The sequence of photographs on these two pages show developments in the design of locomotives from the middle of the last century. Midland and LMS examples will serve to show how locomotives have grown in size. Above left is a Kirtley 2–2–2 passenger engine No 135A of the late 1860s.

[Locomotive Publishing Co

LEFT: One of the same designer's 2–4–0s No 75 of the same period; notice the outside frames and springs.

[Locomotive Publishing Co

LEFT: By the 1880s, Johnson, who had succeeded Kirtley, had cleaned up the exterior lines of his 2–4–0 which was the next development from the Kirtley type above.   [Locomotive Publishing Co

LEFT: The 2–4–0 was enlarged by Johnson in the 1890s into a 4–4–0 with longer boiler and larger driving wheels. These engines were considered by many to be some of the most graceful of late Victorian designs.   [British Railways

RIGHT: The final Fowler development which can be traced through Midland practice was the Royal Scot, first seen in 1927. This was a massive 4–6–0, with large-diameter boiler and minute chimney. During and after the second world war all the Royal Scot 4–6–0s were rebuilt by Stanier.   [Locomotive Publishing Co

RIGHT: Johnson's successor Deeley, and his successor Fowler, rebuilt the Johnson 4-4-0s on more than one occasion and the standard Midland 4-4-0 now looked like this at the time of the grouping in 1923. Principal features were the larger boiler and the footplating carried up over the driving wheels. This particular example lasted into BR days as No 40413.
J. E. Wilkinson

boiler on one side as the exhaust steam is leaving the cylinder on the other side towards the chimney so that a fairly even pull is maintained on the driving wheels. Indeed, a continuous action is built up with steam first on one side of the piston then on the other in quick succession. The driver's reversing lever is used to control the direction of the locomotive by altering the position of the valves in the cylinders but it is also used to control the amount of steam entering the cylinders, since at higher speeds the locomotive needs less steam in the cylinders than when starting from rest.

Although steam locomotives are no longer in use on British Railways numerous examples have been preserved; many are static exhibits in museums but others are in working order, some of which provide the day-to-day motive power on the privately-owned standard gauge railways. On the narrow gauge lines many of the engines in use since the lines were built are still in working order or have been restored to working order after lying derelict. Narrow gauge engines work in very much

the same way as their larger gauge counterparts. What the narrow gauge engines lack in size, although many are much larger than one would expect, they are often of interesting types.

On the Festiniog Railway, for example, apart from conventional locomotives the line also has two types of articulated locomotive. One, known as the Fairlie type, was developed especially for the Festiniog, although it also appeared in other countries. The locomotive consisted of one main frame carrying, in effect, two locomotives. The cab is in the centre and the engine has two boilers, one towards each end, with independent chimneys at the outer ends. The main frame is carried on two bogies, each containing driving wheels and cylinders, thus producing a very powerful locomotive, yet manned by only one crew.

The other unusual type on the Festiniog is a Beyer Garratt locomotive, not in fact built for the Festiniog but in this instance brought back from Tasmania for preservation. It was in fact the first Garratt locomotive to be built by Beyer Peacock,

in 1909 for the 2ft gauge Tasmanian Railways. The Garratt principle was used for many locomotives, particularly in South America, Africa, Australia, and to a much lesser extent in Spain and Britain. The Garratt locomotive consisted of three components, the main boiler and cab assembly mounted on the centre section and two driving wheel units at each end. The driving wheel sections themselves carried water tanks and coal bunker and were pivoted to the outer ends of the centre section in such a way that they could traverse sharp curves.

The main difference between the Garratt and other types of articulated locomotive was that the boiler section was more or less carried between the driving units. This meant that the boiler centre line could be much lower and bigger boilers could be provided. Again very powerful locomotives were produced in this way yet they could run over very light track with sharp curves.

All the locomotives running on the preserved narrow gauge lines were either built for the line in question or have been transferred from closed lines of similar or nearly similar gauge. The Garratt on the Festiniog, for example, was originally built as a 2ft gauge engine and on arrival on the FR its wheels were altered to the slightly narrower 1ft 11½in Festiniog gauge. Thus the choice of locomotives running on the narrow gauge preserved lines is limited to the few engines already on the line or whatever may be available elsewhere.

However, the standard gauge preserved railways are not limited to types which worked over the line when it was owned by British Railways. Indeed, two of the operating standard gauge private railways employ a variety of locomotives of various origins. The Bluebell Railway, for example, described in more detail later, originally part of the LBSCR and later Southern Railway, now houses an interesting collection ranging from diminutive LBSCR Terrier and SECR Class P 0–6–0Ts to a BR Class 4 4–6–0. The Keighley

& Worth Valley Railway collection includes types which regularly or occasionally worked on the branch, including an Ivatt 2–6–2T, an LMS " Crab " 2–6–0 and a Stanier Class 5 4–6–0.

Numerous larger locomotives have been preserved but are not on operating railways with the exception of those housed at Longmoor. Nevertheless, while they cannot run on BR main lines they may occasionally be seen on special occasions in steam at steam galas, running on short lengths of track in private sidings or at museums. It is probably not realised that more than 600 locomotives, including industrial types, are preserved in Great Britain.

Several British Railways main line express locomotives have been preserved for their own sake; the original intention of their new owners was to run them on special excursions over BR tracks but unfortunately the British Railways Board has imposed a total ban on the running of steam locomotives, with one exception; that exception is LNER Class A3 Pacific No 4472 *Flying Scotsman* owned by Alan Pegler, and normally stabled at Doncaster. Mr. Pegler has a contract until 1971 to allow the locomotive to be used on special excursions on various BR routes. The other large preserved locomotives unfortunately cannot be seen on BR metals unless there is a change of attitude by the BRB; they include GW Castle Class 4–6–0 No 4079 *Pendennis Castle*; LNER Class A2 Pacific No 60532 *Blue Peter*; LNER Class A4 Pacifics Nos 60019 *Bittern* and No 4498 *Sir Nigel Gresley*; and Class K4 2–6–0 No 3442.

Although this book is primarily concerned with British preservation ventures we cannot overlook the activities of the Railway Preservation Society of Ireland with its former GNRI Class S 4–4–0 No 171, and former GSWR J15 0–6–0 No 186, both in working order. In Ireland they are more fortunate since these preserved steam locomotives are allowed to run from time to time on NIR and CIE lines.

4 Coaches

COACHES on the early railways of the 1830s and 1840s were little different from road stage coaches; in fact the railway carriage of the period consisted of no more than two or three stagecoach bodies, or compartments as they became known, mounted on a single underframe. Gradually coaches became longer, slightly wider and higher but even by the 1870s the normal British main line coach consisted of four or five compartments and was carried on four or six wheels. Bogie coaches, in which the coach was carried on two pivoted trucks, made their appearance in the 1870s, at first on the Festiniog Railway and very soon after on standard gauge lines. This allowed an increase in length to 40–50ft instead of the 30 or so feet of the average six wheeler. But amenities changed little. Toilets of a sort made their appearance during the 1880s and 1890s and even sleeping cars had been introduced for first class passengers but coaches generally were still without corridors. It was not until the 1890s that corridor trains were introduced, and with them came more extensive use of dining cars. Until that time passengers travelled on the few dining cars for the whole journey unless they changed into and out of dining cars at intermediate stations.

It was not until the early years of the present century that coaches more akin to the size and shape familiar to us were developed with the high semi-elliptical roof and wide bodies built to the full limits of the loading gauge. Indeed, for about 20 years or so around the turn of the century the clerestory roof was popular among carriage designers. This, from its architectural use, was a raised centre section to the roof, with windows on each side of the clerestory deck. This feature allowed more light into the compartment by day. In contrast, however, at night the oil or gas lamp was usually suspended from the clerestory and often cast deep shadows. By 1920 the clerestory roof had been abandoned for new construction and had given way almost without exception to the semi-elliptical roof although some clerestory roofed coaches lasted to the late 1950s in public service on BR. By the 1920s, too, corridor coaches were

RIGHT: Early railway carriages resembled road carriages but with two or three '' bodies '' or compartments as we now know them joined together on one underframe. This early specimen dating from about 1850 originally belonged to the London, Brighton & South Coast Railway but survived on the Isle of Wight until the turn of the century.
[Locomotive Publishing Co

RIGHT LOWER: By the 1870s the style of carriage body had altered and the familiar railway carriage shape was beginning to be seen. Prominent was the panelling around the windows and along the waist, which was to remain in evidence until the end of wooden-bodied coaches in the late 1950s. [British Railways

LEFT: Ones that got away; not all British locomotives which have been preserved are now in the British Isles Several have gone to North America, including SR Schools Class 4–4–0 No 926, LSWR Class M7 0–4–4T No 53 and a GWR corridor brake composite coach, all of which are now displayed at Steamtown USA, in Vermont.   [R. B. Horsley

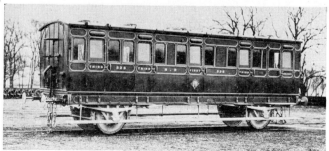

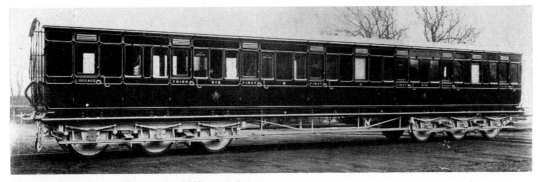

ABOVE: Again taking Midland and LMS examples to show how railway carriages have developed we now see a Midland 12-wheel composite non-corridor coach with luggage compartment and toilet facilities dating from the 1880s for long distance trains.   [British Railways

BELOW: By the end of the last century corridors had made their appearance, and a number of carriage designers used the clerestory roof, that is the raised centre part of the roof with windows along the side, to give more light in the compartment. It dates from about 1908.
[Locomotive Publishing Co

CARRIAGE DEVELOPMEN

general on long-distance main line trains, and to a lesser extent on cross-country services. Very often the latter were provided with non-corridor lavatory stock, that is non-corridor coaches with toilets between compartments, or at one end linked to two or three compartments by short corridors. Non-corridor stock was general on suburban and local services. Timber bodies and underframes were gradually giving way to steel panelled bodies, although retaining timber frames and all-steel underframes, a form of construction which lasted virtually unchanged until the adoption in 1951 of all-steel bodies and framing by British Railways for its standard coaches.

It is unfortunate that the preservation movement

was not formed a little earlier to buy old coaches, since few of the once numerous interesting survivors from the 19th century have been preserved. Most that have been saved are specialised saloons or Royal train vehicles. Indeed there are no ordinary clerestory roof vehicles in original condition and the only examples that have been kept are saloons or departmental vehicles, much altered internally and externally. Yet the Keighley & Worth Valley Railway has managed to acquire stock ranging from four and six-wheeled coaches to modern BR coaches and two BR diesel railbuses.

Although the Kent & East Sussex line, which as this book closes for press, has not so far succeeded in restoring passenger services to the Robertsbridge-

ABOVE: By 1930 the LMS was building large quantities of main line coaches with seats in open saloons. Entrance doors were provided at the coach ends only; notice the similarity of the wooden panelled body to the Midland four-wheeler on page 23.   [British Railways

BELOW: The 1930s was to see a revolution in carriage design in which steel body panels replaced timber. This is one of the LMS Stanier open thirds of the mid-1930s. Each compartment or seating bay had large windows incorporating sliding ventilators, a feature which is still standard today on modern BR coaches.   [British Railways

Tenterden line it has bought a number of narrow-bodied SR corridor coaches originally built for lines with restricted clearances, also a former GWR diesel railcar.

The Bluebell, Severn Valley and Dart Valley lines also have an interesting selection of coaches covering SR, GWR, LMS and Pullman types described later in the chapters on individual lines.

So far as the narrow gauge lines are concerned, like locomotives, coaching stock is generally unique to the line in question. Much of the existing stock, particularly on the Talyllyn and Festiniog, dates back to the opening years. However, both railways have experienced such an increase in traffic that they have built new coaches of modern design and

high seating capacity in the last two or three years. Festiniog stock even includes buffet and observation cars. One of the FR coaches was rebuilt from an old body of a Lynton & Barnstaple coach which lay derelict for many years. The Welshpool & Llanfair Railway added some more stock to the line during 1968 but the vehicles were not new. Indeed, they were not even British for they came from the Zillertalbahn in Austria which is of similar gauge. Naturally coaches of narrow gauge lines are not as high or wide as those on standard gauge lines but even the RHDR 15in gauge coaches can seat two passengers side by side and convey them at speeds of up to 25mph, an exciting prospect on such a narrow gauge.

5 Signalling

IN THE early days of railways signalling was a very haphazard affair. Each station would have its signalman, at one time known as a policeman since the early railways followed very much the pattern of roads. The signalman controlled the points and signals but there was one big drawback, the fact that there was no means of communication between the signalmen at adjacent stations. Trains were operated on the time interval system; after the passage of one train the signals at the station it had just passed were kept at danger for about 5min. They were then placed in the caution position so that should another train pass through the station the driver would be warned that he was only about 5min behind the train in front. But if no train passed, after about a further 5min the signalman would place the signals in the clear position. Nevertheless, there was no guarantee that because the signals were in the clear position that the line in fact was clear. Ten minutes might have elapsed since the passage of the previous train but there was always the possibility that it could have stopped

no more than a mile or so along the line having broken down. Thus a second train running under clear signals might easily come across the stranded train perhaps hidden by a curve and no more than about 100yd or so ahead and not be able to stop before running into it.

At the same time as the development of the early railways the electric telegraph was being perfected. By the 1860s some railways had realised the value of the telegraph for sending messages between stations about the running of trains. But it was not until the Regulation of Railways Act in 1889 that all railways were compelled to adopt the block telegraph system. In this system the line was divided into a series of block sections, generally the section of line between two stations or between two signal boxes if intermediate signalboxes existed at junctions or elsewhere without a station. The block principle was established that there should not be more than one train in one block section on one line at one time. This was achieved by using the electric telegraph for sending messages between signalboxes so that signalmen knew when trains entered and left a section.

Although the early telegraph system used spelt-out messages in code form, for railway purposes this was too cumbersome and bell signals were used instead in which codes on a single stroke bell denoted the type of train and the various other messages that were required to be sent. A needle indicator was used as well to show the state of the block section. In later years this became a three-position instrument with the needle pointing vertically to a panel marked " line blocked ", deflected diagonally one way to another panel marked " line clear " and the other way to a panel

FAR LEFT: Until the mid-1920s nearly all signal arms in Britain were lowered from the horizontal danger position to the clear indication. This is an LSW type signal still in use on the Southern Railway in 1946.

[British Railways

NEARER LEFT: The Great Northern Railway and several other companies in Britain adopted signals known as the somersault type in which the arms were separately pivoted from the coloured glass spectacles. [P. J. Lynch

marked " train on line ". This is still the basis of block signalling today where mechanical signalling survives on British Railways.

The procedure is quite simple. Assuming there is no train in the section the signalman at the signalbox A presses his bell tapper once which rings the bell once in box B. This is the call attention signal. The signalman at box B replies with one beat on the bell, after which signalman A sends, for example, four beats on the bell (Is line clear for an express passenger train?). If the block section is clear and for a distance, usually ¼ mile, beyond signalman B's first stop signal, signalman B replies with four beats on the bell and places the block indicator for the A-B section at " line clear ". Signalman A can then clear his signals for the train to proceed. When the train leaves or passes signalbox A the signalman there sends two beats on the bell to box B (train entering section), which B acknowledges with two beats and places the block indicator at " train on line ". The block indicator needles by the way are displayed in both signalboxes A and B so that both signalmen can see the state of the line. Now signalman B goes through the same procedure to the next box ahead at C, offering the train by the bell; if it is accepted he clears his signals. As the train passes signalbox B the signalman there sends the " train entering section " signal to C. If all is well with the train and the signalman at B is satisfied that it is complete with its tail lamp he replaces his signals to danger behind the train and calls the attention of A with one beat on the bell. When A acknowledges this signal signalman B sends two-pause-one beats on the bell (train out of section) and places

the block indicator for section A-B at " line blocked ". The signalman at A returns the two-pause-one bell signal, after which the section is free to be used for the next train should it be ready to leave A.

The block system became standard on all double-track lines but something more was needed on single lines to avoid any possibility of a head-on collision. At first a pilotman was used, that is a man appointed specially to accompany each train through the block section. Clearly this was wasteful of manpower and eventually a symbol replaced the pilotman. This symbol was in the form of a wooden staff. There is only one staff for each single-line block section and since a driver must carry the staff for the section concerned before his train can leave a passing place, head-on collisions should, in theory, be impossible.

BELOW: Diagram showing block working between signal boxes A, B, C and D, and in the lower diagram simple single line operation.

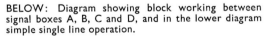

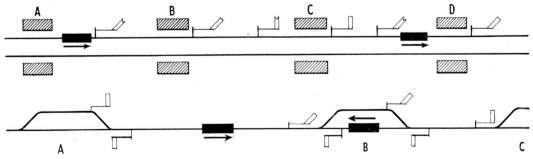

With only one staff it meant that trains had to run alternately in opposite directions, clearly an inflexible situation. To overcome this difficulty the staff and ticket system was devised. If several consecutive trains had to pass over the single line section in the same direction each train except the last in the group was given a written ticket authorising the driver to proceed through the section. As he was given the ticket the driver was also shown the staff. The last train of the group carried the staff and until the signalman at the opposite end of the section received the staff he could not send any trains the other way.

Another method where traffic was light was the divisible staff where the one staff for the section could be unscrewed into two or even three sections. Each part of the staff was given to following trains in the same direction but again the signalman at the other end could not despatch any trains in the opposite direction until he had received all the parts of the staff.

Even these systems were often inflexible, particularly when trains were running late and out of order. There are many stories of station masters or porters having to cycle from one end of the section to the other with the staff, or send it by taxi, or, in the days before road vehicles, by horse, during which time passengers in a waiting train fumed. As a result the electric staff was developed. In this system special block instruments were devised, one in each of the signalboxes at both ends of a single line section. The block instruments contained a number of single line staffs but the two instruments were so interlocked electrically that only one staff could be obtained from either instrument at one time. The block signalling procedure was used so far as the bell signals were concerned but as the signalman at B returned the " line clear " signal to signalbox A the signalman held his bell tapper down on the last beat, which action released the lock on the staff instrument at A allowing the signalman at A to withdraw the staff. Once this had been done no other staff could be obtained until the first staff had been put in the instrument at B, or at A if the train did not proceed for any reason. The electric staff was a long metal rod with rings round it so that it would fit only into the instruments for which it was designed. This was rather a cumbersome thing to carry around and indeed it was very heavy when being handed up from a signalman to the driver of a passing train, even though speed was limited to 10mph. Smaller versions of the electric staff were developed, including the tablet (a round flat disc), the miniature staff, and in recent years the key token, no more than about 1ft long. Because of their small size the latter three were placed in a leather pouch attached to a hoop for hand exchange between driver and signalman.

All the preserved and private light railways, with the exception of the Romney Hythe & Dymchurch, operate on single lines and therefore must have some form of staff system. The RHDR uses a form of double-line block working in which the block signalling messages are sent over a telephone. The single line controls on the other private rail-

LEFT: The driver of Talyllyn Railway No 2 *Dolgoch* takes the staff from the signalman for the single line section from Towyn Pendre towards Abergynolwyn on July 3, 1968.   [G. F. Gillham

RIGHT: The Science Museum has acquired an original British Railways signalbox from Haddiscoe Junction, including lamps and stove. Although the complete lever frame has not been installed several different types of signalling equipment are displayed inside the signalbox.   [Science Museum

ways employ one or other of the staff or token systems but those using the simplest forms, that is the one-engine-in-steam staff or the divisible staff, are finding that with increased traffic more flexible operation is needed to allow the running of additional trains at short notice.

Although many of the private railways are operated by enthusiast bodies, with amateur railwaymen, in no sense is railway operation an amateur affair. All operating staff whether on the footplate, in the signalbox or on a station, are thoroughly competent operators who must satisfy the operating company that they know the rules and regulations for train operation and signalling. Many, of course, are professional railwaymen who love railways for their own sake and find relaxation in helping to run the surviving steam lines, in contrast to the hurly-burly of a modern main line system. Indeed, before the Ministry of Transport grants authority in the form of a Light Railway Order to run passenger services it must be satisfied that the railway will operate to established standards.

Although the pace of our privately-owned standard gauge and narrow gauge lines may be slow, with ageing steam locomotives and rolling stock employed on many trains, the running of a private railway cannot be undertaken in a haphazard fashion. Indeed, with recent yearly passenger totals on some lines at over 300,000 the total number of passengers carried by all the private railways in Britain in one year is over the million mark. Without the activities of hardworking railway enthusiasts these picturesque railways and the steam locomotive would be all but extinct in this country. With your support and their enthusiasm let us hope they can keep running for many years to come. In the following chapters we describe the operating railways and static museums in more detail area by area.

ABOVE: Two locomotives from the national collection, GNR Atlantics Nos 990 and 251, were brought out of retirement in York Museum in 1953 to work special excursions to mark the centenary of Doncaster Works.   [R. E. Vincent]

PART TWO—PRESERVATION

6 *The National collection*

THERE IS nothing new in railway preservation, hence the survival of such items as Stephenson's *Rocket* in the Science Museum, London, the 1830 *Invicta* at Canterbury, together with *Locomotion* (1825) and *Derwent* (1845) at Darlington among many other older-timers preserved. In the last few years the contracting railway scene and modernisation of what is left have brought about the disappearance of many once-familiar railway items, not least the steam engine. Inevitably this has led to a tremendous upsurge of interest in preservation, and in some cases a desperate urge to preserve items regardless of historical interest or importance, hence some inevitable duplication. As a result no fewer than 10 LBSCR Stroudley Terrier 0-6-0Ts survive with as many LMS Stanier Class 5 4-6-0s. In retrospect one can

only wish that preservation had been continued on a more consistent basis over the years so that some items destroyed at a time when there was no interest might still survive for us today.

In fact locomotive preservation suffered two setbacks at the hands of Swindon engineers. Until 1906 *North Star*, which hauled the first GWR train out of Paddington in 1838, survived at Swindon, together with the 8ft single-wheeler *Lord of the Isles* of 1851. Churchward decreed that they took up valuable space and they were scrapped. The driving wheels of *Lord of the Isles* survive in Swindon Museum, as also does a replica of *North Star* built at some expense as part of the 1925 S&DR centenary celebrations. Stanier, who once served under Churchward at Swindon, made a similar decision on arrival at Derby in 1932. As a

ABOVE: Many of the British transport museums are not rail connected and locomotives have to be moved by road trailer; GWR Castle class 4–6–0 No 4073 *Caerphilly Castle* is seen here on its way to the Science Museum, London.
[R. C. Riley

RIGHT: One of the first locomotives to be preserved privately was LBSCR 0–4–2 *Gladstone*, bought by the SLS in 1927 and exhibited in York Museum.

BELOW: GW 4–4–0 No 3717 *City of Truro* is eased off a Pickfords low-loader into Swindon Museum, its final resting place, on April 15, 1962.
[M. Pope

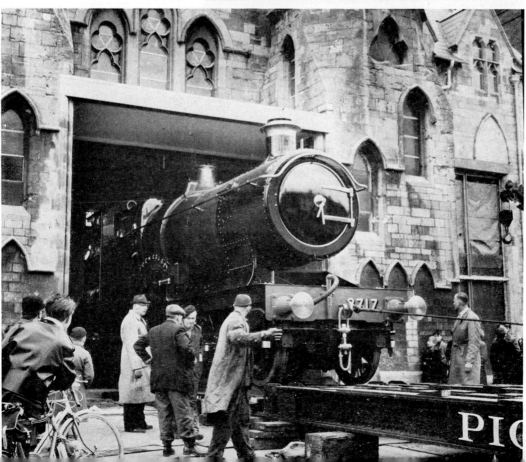

ABOVE: One of the most ornate liveries to be seen on a preserved locomotive is that of SE&CR Class D 4–4–0 No 737, preserved at Clapham Museum. [G. M. Kichenside

result, three preserved Midland Railway engines, Kirtley 0–6–0 goods engine No 421 of 1856, his 2–4–0 No 156A of 1866 and Johnson's first 0–4–4T, No 6 of 1875, were broken up. Another casualty was North London Railway 4–4–0T No 6 of 1868 vintage. The only Midland Railway survivor was the 4–2–2 express engine No 118 built in 1897. Perhaps it was more than even Stanier dared to scrap the LNWR relics at Crewe; probably they survived because there was more room available than at Derby. Stanier later became less opposed to preserving the past, for in the mid-

1930s Caledonian Railway 4–2–2 No 123 of 1886 and Highland Railway "Jones Goods" 4–6–0 No 103 of 1894 were preserved and restored to their old liveries.

In contrast to the LMS, the LNER pursued a more enlightened policy. It had celebrated the centenary of the Stockton & Darlington Railway in 1925 in a big way and subsequently established a railway museum on part of the site of the old station at York. Its contents are largely from the constituent companies of the LNER, but exceptions include LNWR 2–2–2 Columbine of 1845

BELOW: Another of the Clapham locomotives is LNWR 2–4–0 No 790 Hardwicke.   [British Railways

ABOVE: Festiniog Railway Fairlie 0–4–4–0T *Earl of Merioneth* heads a train from Tan-y-Bwlch to Portmadoc at Minffordd.
[S. Evans

BELOW: Welshpool & Llanfair 0–6–0T *The Earl* heads a special train over the Banwy bridge between Castle Caereinion and Llanfair Caereinion on April 7, 1968.
[D. Huntriss

ABOVE: Bluebell Railway Adams 4–4–2T No 488 heads
a train composed of LNW, SEC and LSW stock from
Sheffield Park to Horsted Keynes in June 1966.
[J. A. C. Kirke

ABOVE: In the collection of rolling stock at Clapham are a number of Royal saloons. This is the interior of Queen Alexandra's saloon built by the LNWR in 1903. [British Railways

RIGHT: Queen Adelaide's bed carriage of the London & Birmingham Railway, built in 1842. This was a typical first class carriage of the period with one half and two full compartments. The compartment at the far end of the coach could be converted into sleeping accommodation by placing stretchers across the seats. Because the compartment was little more than 5ft between partitions a flap in the coach end could be opened to allow the royal feet to extend into the carriage boot. [British Railways

and LBSC 0–4–2 *Gladstone* of 1882, the latter preserved in 1927 as the successful outcome of a fund organised by the Stephenson Locomotive Society.

The outbreak of war in 1939 stopped further preservation and some engines that might otherwise have survived were broken up, the most notable being Isle of Wight Railway 2–4–0T *Ryde* of 1864. After the war the railways went through a difficult time. Nevertheless the SLS took the initiative in drawing attention to the desirability of preserving certain engines and their efforts continued after nationalisation, culminating in 1951 in the appointment by the BTC of Mr. John Scholes as Curator of Historical Relics. Several engines were preserved at this time, including MR Kirtley 2–4–0 No 158A, replacing one of the designs axed by Stanier. In 1956 the centenary of the London, Tilbury & Southend Railway was celebrated with a special

train hauled by that company's 4–4–2T No 80 *Thundersley* restored to original livery. A former LTSR coach restored at the same time was broken up at Stratford the following year without authority, together with a GER tram engine and coach. Once more this focussed attention on the fact that items preserved and thought safe might be disposed of at the whim of one man, and fears were expressed as to the future of other preserved stock stored in BR workshops.

In 1958 representatives of the SLS, the Railway Club and the Historical Model Railway Society met Sir Brian Robertson, Chairman of the BTC. He proved sympathetic to the cause of preservation and agreed to the establishment of a number of regional museums, making use of existing buildings to cut down cost. He also wished to be kept informed of the interests of the various societies and so came into being the Consultative Panel for the

In 1956, to mark the centenary of the London, Tilbury & Southend line, British Railways restored former LTSR 4–4–2T No 80 *Thundersley* and an LTSR coach into their original liveries. The locomotive survives and is displayed at Bressingham Hall. The coach, although stored for preservation, was later broken up. The locomotive and coach are seen above on one of the centenary specials.

[R. E. Vincent

LEFT: A general view of York Railway Museum showing, nearest the camera on the left, LBSCR 0–4–2 *Gladstone*

[T. A. Imbush

BELOW: Among the Clapham collection is the holder of the world's speed record for steam traction, LNER Class A4 Pacific No 4468 *Mallard*.

[R. C. Riley

Preservation of British Transport Relics, which has met regularly ever since and on which most national rail and road transport societies are represented. Early in 1961 the small exhibits' section of the new Clapham Museum was opened, followed in 1963 by the whole collection. Before his BTC appointment Mr. Scholes was Curator of the Castle Museum, York, which while having no direct transport associations is widely known as one of the finest displays of its kind. Now he had applied this remarkable flair to the arrangement of some of the most important relics in the national transport collection and the result was magnificent. In less than six years Clapham Museum has gained the reputation of being the finest transport museum in Europe, if not in the world.

Meanwhile another museum had opened at Swindon, and more recently others at Glasgow and Leicester. The former is partly administered by the local corporation, the two others are wholly so administered. This left BR with the sole responsibility for the museums at Clapham and York. However, since the transport museums could not be self-supporting they were singled out by Dr. Beeching for closure and to relieve BR of this continuing burden the latest Transport Act transfers responsibility for them to the Department of Education and Science. It has now been decreed that both Clapham and York museums must close and that such part of the collection as can be accommodated will be placed in a new museum converted from part of York Motive Power Depot, the advantage of rail connection being one reason suggested for this move. Since BR will not allow steam locomotives to run on its tracks this advantage seems obscure. There has been considerable public outcry over the proposed closure of Clapham Museum, but so far to no avail. Its contents may present a cold and silent contrast to their once noisy vitality but nevertheless the collection should be visited and visited again while it is still intact. The exhibits are so many and varied that only some of the highlights can be mentioned. Among the engines are *Mallard*, the LNER Class A4 Pacific that holds the World's speed record for steam, one of the famous Midland Compound 4–4–0s, LSWR Adams " High Flyer " 4–4–0

No 563 of 1893, a Great Central Director 4–4–0, LNWR 2–2–2 *Cornwall* of 1847 and 2–4–0 *Hardwicke* of 1892 and many more. Among the coaches pride of place goes to the royal saloons, but there are many others, while the small exhibits are no less fascinating. As a general transport museum there are also several trams and buses, but London Transport has made it clear that when Clapham closes its own exhibits will not leave London and will go into store, no longer on public view. There are already a number of engines in store awaiting exhibition, and the compression of the contents of Clapham and York into a smaller museum can only mean that more of the national collection will remain unseen. It is a saddening thought that indifference in high places to our national transport heritage has led to the threat to disperse this magnificent collection of incalculable value as an educational medium.

Among other important items in the national collection to be seen elsewhere are the pioneer GWR Castle 4–6–0, *Caerphilly Castle* of 1923, at the Science Museum, London and LMS Coronation 4–6–2 *City of Birmingham*, built in 1939, at the Birmingham Museum of Science and Industry. Until a new Transport Museum is built at Leicester four preserved engines have been temporarily housed in the old Stoneygate Tram Depot 2½ miles south of the city. Here are the Midland 4–2–2 and 2–4–0 already mentioned, an early 600V d c electric locomotive built for the NER in 1904 and an 0–4–0ST built in 1906 by the Brush Engineering Co, Loughborough. Eventually Leicester is likely to provide homes for the LNER Gresley 2–6–2 *Green Arrow*, a Great Central Railway 2–8–0 and LNWR 0–8–0 among others. York Museum houses several NER engines, 2–2–4T *Aerolite*, built 1851 but much rebuilt subsequently, a long boilered 0–6–0 of 1874 and 2–4–0 and 4–4–0 express engines of 1885 and 1893 respectively. The pioneer GNR Atlantic No 990 *Henry Oakley* of 1898 and its large-boilered successor No 251 of 1902 make an interesting contrast with GNR No 1, a Stirling single of 1870. Some of the other large exhibits in York have already been mentioned in the text, while those of Swindon and Glasgow are detailed in the appropriate chapters.

7 Wales

PRIVATE railway preservation dates back only to 1951 when the Talyllyn Railway Preservation Society was formed and took over operation of the moribund line. Talyllyn history goes back to 1865, when slate traffic was first carried, passenger traffic commencing the following year. The two engines *Talyllyn* (1865) and *Dolgoch* (1866) provided the sole motive power to deal with the line's life blood—the slate traffic from Bryn Eglwys quarry—and such passenger traffic as there was. In 1946 the quarry closed and from then on the line had to rely entirely on summer tourist traffic. In fact it had been closed entirely for a time during

the previous year when *Dolgoch* was sent away for overhaul and *Talyllyn* was worked to a standstill. In the summer of 1949, too, traffic was suspended for a while to enable essential repairs to be carried out on *Dolgoch*. The railway owed its somewhat precarious existence to the interest of Sir Haydn Jones, who had acquired control in 1911, but on his death in the summer of 1950 it became abundantly clear that the railway, too, would perish at the end of the season unless something was done.

Hence the formation of the first Preservation Society to take over a railway. With only one engine, *Dolgoch*, in working order it was necessary

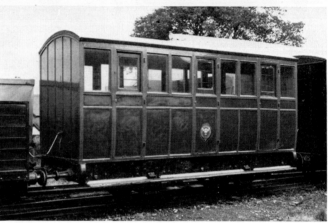

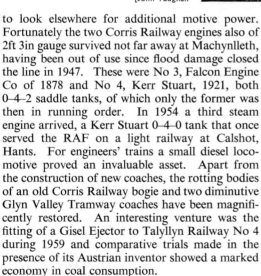

ABOVE: Traffic has increased on the Welsh narrow gauge lines to such an extent that new coaches have been built in the past few years; this is a new bogie coach of the Talyllyn Railway.

RIGHT: Some of the original Talyllyn four-wheelers still survive and although they are still used from time to time they are not used in everyday service because of the need to preserve them in good condition. [P. J. Sharpe

LEFT: Heavy traffic on Easter Monday 1968 resulted in the operation of this double-headed train on the Talyllyn, the 1.15p.m. from Towyn to Abergynolwyn, worked by engines *Talyllyn* and *Douglas*; the train is seen near Dolgoch.

[John Vaughan

to look elsewhere for additional motive power. Fortunately the two Corris Railway engines also of 2ft 3in gauge survived not far away at Machynlleth, having been out of use since flood damage closed the line in 1947. These were No 3, Falcon Engine Co of 1878 and No 4, Kerr Stuart, 1921, both 0–4–2 saddle tanks, of which only the former was then in running order. In 1954 a third steam engine arrived, a Kerr Stuart 0–4–0 tank that once served the RAF on a light railway at Calshot, Hants. For engineers' trains a small diesel locomotive proved an invaluable asset. Apart from the construction of new coaches, the rotting bodies of an old Corris Railway bogie and two diminutive Glyn Valley Tramway coaches have been magnificently restored. An interesting venture was the fitting of a Gisel Ejector to Talyllyn Railway No 4 during 1959 and comparative trials made in the presence of its Austrian inventor showed a marked economy in coal consumption.

Apart from the pleasant hill scenery of the seven-

mile line as it climbs from Towyn to Abergynolwyn, there is the attraction of Dolgoch Falls, while for those prepared to walk further afield there is Talyllyn Lake, from which the line gets its name. Beside the Wharf station at Towyn there is the Narrow Gauge Museum, started under TR auspices but now administered by a separate trust. Here there is a fine collection of small relics of the narrow gauge together with several locomotives, of which the metre gauge *Cambrai* built in France in 1888 is perhaps the most interesting.

The TRPS has a strong and active membership and can be proud of its achievements, which have been faithfully recorded over many years in 60 issues of the *Talyllyn News*. This magazine and the annual accounts of the railway should be compulsory reading for all would-be preservationists for herein every pound spent is accounted for and the cost of keeping a seven-mile narrow gauge line functioning is quite an eye-opener. Each year operating profits and society funds are ploughed

ABOVE: The Festiniog Railway stock includes a buffet car in which draught beer is served. This coach was extensively reconditioned from an old Lynton & Barnstaple coach body which had been used for many years as a chicken shed.

LEFT: An unusual vehicle on the Festiniog Railway is the observation car, which includes armchairs in the saloon.

FESTINIOG COACHING STOCK

LEFT: Coach preservation has its problems, particularly with rotten timber which must be stripped out and replaced. This is one of the original FR bogie coaches, seen under reconstruction at Boston Lodge works in 1961.

BELOW: The careful restoration of preserved coaches is clearly seen in the fine condition of this original Festiniog bogie composite.

into the railway so providing ever improving facilities for the visitor—a record 122,000 passenger journeys were achieved in 1968.

As the Talyllyn goes from strength to strength, so too does its neighbour further up the Cambrian Coast. The Festiniog Railway was authorised by Act of Parliament as far back as 1832, and was opened throughout from Blaenau Festiniog to Portmadoc four years later. At first horses were responsible for haulage of the slate traffic that was the line's *raison d'etre*, but as traffic increased it became clear that some narrow gauge steam engines would have to be designed. These were four 0–4–0 tanks built at George England's South London works in 1863–4 and three still survive, although only *Prince* is fit for traffic. These little engines, good as they were, could not handle the increasingly heavy loads and a solution was provided by an engineer named Fairlie, who designed a double four-coupled engine unit *Little Wonder* that proved twice as powerful as its predecessors. It was not an unqualified success but during its short life demonstrated the advantages of the design, while modifications in later engines avoided the failings of the prototype. Two such engines are still at work, *Merddin Emrys* of 1879 and *Earl of Merioneth* of 1885, both built by the FR in its Boston Lodge works.

The Festiniog Railway would perhaps have pursued as uneventful a course as the Talyllyn, had it not been for its association with the insolvent Welsh Highland Railway in the years preceeding the second world war. As a result it lost thousands of pounds that it could ill afford. A journey on the Welsh Highland must have been an unforgettable experience for it passed through outstandingly beautiful mountain scenery, but latterly apart from a few summer tourists traffic was negligible. Despite Festiniog help it closed in 1937; four years later the track was lifted and sold for scrap. One of its engines, *Russell*, a Hunslet 2–6–2T of 1906 survives in the hands of the Welsh Highland Preservation Society, a body that plans eventually to restore a short length of track, but this can never recapture the thrill of the 21-mile journey from Portmadoc, through the Aberglaslyn Pass to meet the LNWR line at Dinas Junction. The Festiniog Railway survived the war, when enemy action meant an increased demand for its important slate traffic. Its passenger traffic ceased at the close of the 1939 summer and in 1946 the freight traffic was finally withdrawn.

One can only be thankful it did not succumb earlier, when it might have been torn up to aid the war effort. Instead the line was left just as it was after the last train ran, its engines rusting away, its stock damaged by vandals, its track becoming more and more overgrown. Although its 1ft 11½in gauge was less than that of the Talyllyn its trackwork and rolling stock were larger and heavier, while its line was 13½ miles in length.

In 1954 Mr. A. F. Pegler obtained control of the company by purchase of its shares, a new board of directors was appointed and the Festiniog Railway Society Ltd was formed to provide the volunteer labour and financial assistance so necessary to restore the line. Next year a short service ran across The Cob between Portmadoc and Boston Lodge, extended in 1956 to Minffordd. The 1958 season saw seven miles of line open as far as Tan-y-Bwlch, and over 60,000 passengers were carried. It was no longer possible to reach Blaenau Festiniog over the old track because the Electricity Board had built a reservoir engulfing part of the line, near Moelwyn Tunnel, an appeal against this having proved abortive. Undiscouraged, the FR obtained a light railway amendment order for a deviation line and an immense amount of work has already been undertaken towards the building of a new line by an alternative route on higher ground above the reservoir. In 1968 the line was extended to Dduallt, 9½ miles from Portmadoc, at which point the deviation begins. It will be many years before Blaenau is reached again, but meanwhile its members have something to aim for and the company can be proud of its successful achievements to date, an impressive 294,000 passenger journeys having been recorded in 1968.

The FR traveller has much to enjoy. There is the sheer delight of the passing scene with the contrast of the coast at Portmadoc and wild mountain country beyond Tan-y-Bwlch, the line running on a ledge on the steep hillside, with impressive views before and after Garnedd Tunnel. The saloon coaches, of which several are new, are particularly smooth running, while there is the added attraction of the only buffet car in the country where *draught* beer is served! Motive power now is provided by *Prince*, the two double Fairlies, *Merddin Emrys* and *Earl of Merioneth*, two four-coupled saddle tanks from the Penrhyn Railway, *Linda* and *Blanche*, built by Hunslet of Leeds in 1893, and *Mountaineer* a 1917 built American 2–6–2T, acquired after war service in France by the Tramway de Pithiviers à Toury, and brought to Wales after the 1964 closure of that line. The type is no stranger to this country—one example survived on the Welsh Highland until 1941.

STEAM
IN
WALES

ABOVE: The spectacular location of the upper reaches of the Festiniog Railway is amply seen in this photograph of 0–4–0ST *Blanche* photographed near Garnedd tunnel between Tan-y-Bwlch and Dduallt.   [R. C. Riley

ABOVE RIGHT: A picturesque view of Festiniog 0–4–4–0T *Earl of Merioneth* leaving Boston Lodge on April 8, 1968.   [Jack Patience

RIGHT: British Railways' only narrow gauge line, and indeed its only steam line, is that between Aberystwyth and Devils Bridge; 2–6–2T No 9 *Prince of Wales* leaves Aberystwyth for Devils Bridge on July 3, 1968.
[G. F. Gillham

FAR RIGHT: Welshpool & Llanfair 0–6–0T No 2 *The Countess* runs alongside the Banwy river near Heniarth on September 14, 1968.   The loading coach is one of the former Zillertalbahn coaches recently acquired by the W&L.   [Allan Stewart

ABOVE: On a fine day some spectacular views can be
obtained from the Snowdon Mountain Railway. Two
trains are seen climbing towards the summit of the line
on July 30, 1965.   [Malcolm Dunnett

Unique in this country is the independent Snowdon Mountain Railway, a rack type railway from
Llanberis which climbs nearly 3,500ft above sea
level and so offers splendid views of the surrounding
mountains. The Abt rack system involves the use
of cogwheels on the locomotive engaging with
toothed rails, in the centre of the track. The system
is much used in Switzerland, where the line's
locomotives were built. First opened on Easter
Monday 1896, the line closed the same day after an
accident involving engine No 1 *Ladas*, which was
damaged beyond repair. The line reopened a year
later after additional safeguards were provided.
The 2ft 7½in gauge engines are all 0–4–2Ts and
Enid, *Wyddfa*, *Snowdon* and *Moel Siabod* remain of
the original stock, while *Padarn*, *Aylwin* and *Eryri*
were added in 1922–3. The line is 5¾ miles long
and the steepest gradient is 1 in 5½. Trains run on
weekdays in the spring and summer months only,
and on certain peak Sundays; the journey lasts an
hour each way.

The Industrial Locomotive Society in collabora-
tion with the National Trust has established a small
locomotive museum at Penrhyn Castle, near
Bangor. Here can be found one of the 0–6–2
" coal tanks " once so familiar a sight on the
LNWR, and long associated with its Welsh lines.
Industrial locomotives include a Neilson 0–4–0WT
of 1870 from Beckton Gasworks, East London,
Charles, a Hunslet 0–4–0ST of 1882 from Penrhyn
Quarries, and a Black Hawthorn 0–4–0ST of 1879
from Kettering Ironworks. Here, too, is one of
the nameboards from Llanfairpwllgwyngyllgo-
gerychwyrndrobwllllantysiliogogogoch   on   the
Bangor-Holyhead line.

Another independent line in Wales is the two
mile 15in gauge line from Fairbourne to Penrhyn
Point connecting with the ferry across the
Mawddach estuary to Barmouth. This line
operates daily in the summer months and spent
the first 25 years of its existence as a 2ft gauge
horse tramway. In 1916, following a similar con-

version then taking place on the Ravenglass & Eskdale Railway, the old established firm of Bassett-Lowke was called in to convert the line to 15in gauge worked by miniature steam engines. Many engines have worked the line since then but the present stud consists of two 2–4–2s, *Katie* and *Sian*, built in recent years but looking older since they have some characteristics of GWR engines of the Dean era, a 4–4–2 *Count Louis* and some small but adequate diesel locomotives.

A few years after the Talyllyn and Festiniog Railways had become established the opportunity arose for a Preservation Society to acquire a third Welsh narrow gauge line. This was the 2ft 6in gauge Welshpool & Llanfair line. From the outset in 1903 the W & L was closely associated with the Cambrian Railways and when the latter company was merged into the GWR in 1922 it was clear that its independent days were numbered. It, too, was absorbed a year later and in 1931 passenger traffic ceased, the freight service surviving until 1956. A Society was then formed and after lengthy negotiations with BR obtained permission to start clearance work on the line. In 1961 *The Earl*, one of the line's two engines returned after five years' absence to be joined in 1962 by *Countess*. Four miles of the line from Llanfair to Castle Caereinion reopened in 1963, extended 1¼ miles to Sylfaen the following year, when unfortunately the bridge over the River Banwy was damaged by floods. With help from the Royal Engineers the bridge was repaired and a serious setback overcome.

Apart from the two original engines, the line uses *Nutty*, an unusual 1929 built Sentinel steam engine from the London Brick Company, *Monarch*, an equally unusual articulated locomotive built by Bagnall in 1953 for Bowater Lloyds' line at Sittingbourne, and two diesels. The first passenger coaches used by the Society originated on the Chattenden & Upnor Railway in Kent, but in 1968 four coaches from the Austrian Zillertalbahn arrived after a lengthy journey, including the Ostend-Dover channel crossing. Three of these coaches are of 1900–1 vintage, the fourth was built in 1925 for the Salzkammergut Lokalbahn. Passenger traffic is substantially less than that of the other Welsh lines but may improve in 1970, when it is hoped that the line will penetrate Welshpool, its original terminus, once more.

BR steams on in Wales with nearly 12 miles of narrow gauge between Aberystwyth and Devils Bridge. This 1ft 11½in gauge line started life in 1902 as the Vale of Rheidol Light Railway. As with its narrow gauge neighbours on the Cambrian Coast it is hard to realise now that the Rheidol line was built primarily for freight traffic, for which it opened a few months before it carried passengers. It soon became apparent that it was benefiting tourists in the summer months. Since there were only 12 carriages, more than adequate in winter, the company suspended timber traffic during the height of summer during which its six bogie timber trucks were modified to serve as open passenger vehicles. Came the fall and they reverted to their normal use! In 1913 the Cambrian Railways acquired the share capital and the line lost its independence, but the mineral traffic was declining and ceased altogether after the first world war. The GWR withdrew the winter passenger service in 1930 and goods traffic ceased seven years later. The 1939–45 war saw all trains suspended but the summer service was resumed in 1945 and has continued ever since.

The Vale of Rheidol line is one of outstanding beauty. As far as Capel Bangor gradients are easy but for the remaining seven miles the line is predominantly climbing on a grade of 1 in 50, until Devils Bridge is reached, 680ft above sea level. Although it deserves to succeed as much as the other Welsh narrow gauge lines it has never done so, largely through a lack of imaginative publicity. Indeed BR is so obsessed with its modern image that it seems slightly self-conscious about continuing to own three steam engines, even if it has adorned them in rail blue. To cut costs passing loops have been removed and the line diverted into the main station at Aberystywth. Nevertheless there remains a strong feeling that BR may dispose of the line as a going concern. The engines are 2–6–2 tanks and *Prince of Wales* is one of the two original engines of 1902, while *Owain Glyndŵr* and *Llywelyn* were built to the same design at Swindon in 1923. Whoever its owners may be the line is always worth a visit in the summer months and at the time of writing has the unique feature of BR still in steam!

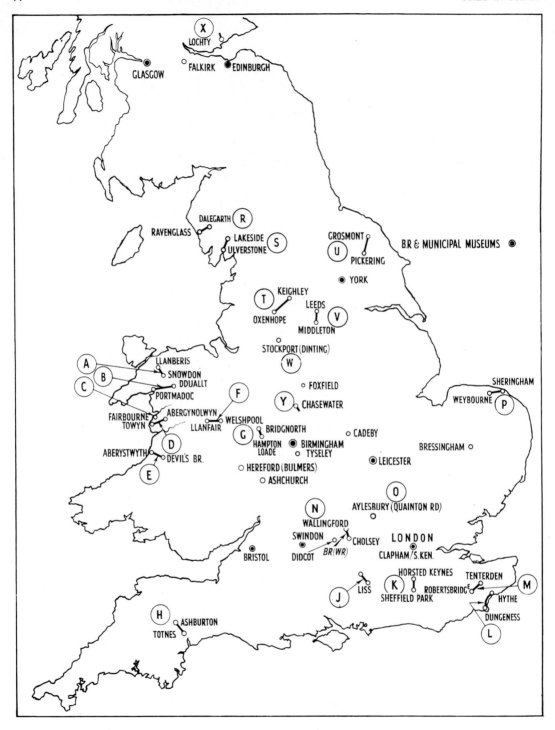

8 *South and West*

MOST POPULAR venue in the south for the steam enthusiast is the Bluebell Line, an attractive five-mile branch in East Sussex. It once formed part of the line from Lewes to East Grinstead. Early preservation attempts envisaged the retention of the whole line, but apart from the difficulties of operating 20 miles of line, the three miles out of Lewes were still operated by BR as part of the Lewes-Tunbridge Wells service, as also was East Grinstead station. As a compromise the Bluebell Railway Preservation Society obtained a lease of the five miles of single track between Sheffield Park and Horsted Keynes, although until the 1962 season its trains did not regularly enter the latter station, instead using a halt platform outside. Opened in 1882, the line closed in 1955, but owing to a legal loophole was reopened in 1956, a minimum service operating until final closure two years later.

Under the Preservation Society it reopened in 1960 with two coaches and two engines and since there was no run-round at the halt and trains could not be propelled, the entire rolling stock of the line had to be used for each train that season, which to the end of October brought the remarkable total of 15,000 passengers. The two engines were LBSC "Terrier" 0–6–0 tank No 55 *Stepney* of 1875 and an equally small SECR Class P 0–6–0T built in 1910 named *Bluebell*. Incredible to realise now, the diminutive "Terriers" were designed to work what would today be termed commuter trains in the South London suburbs; their SECR counterparts were primarily intended for country branch lines and shunting at the Channel ports.

In 1961 two more engines arrived, a second

LEFT: Map showing the location of the privately-operated preserved railways and the principal museums and depots. Not all the private lines are in operation at present. **A** Snowdon Mountain Railway; **B** Festiniog Railway; **C** Fairbourne Railway; **D** Talyllyn Railway; **E** British Railways' Vale of Rheidol line; **F** Welshpool & Llanfair Railway; **G** Severn Valley Railway; **H** Dart Valley Railway; **J** Longmoor Military Railway; **K** Bluebell Railway; **L** Romney Hythe & Dymchurch Railway; **M** Kent & East Sussex Railway; **N** GW Society (Wallingford branch BR); **O** Quainton Road depot of the London RPS; **P** Midland & Great Northern Railway Preservation Society; **R** Ravenglass & Eskdale Railway; **S** Lakeside Railway; **T** Keighley & Worth Valley Railway; **U** North Yorkshire Moors RPS; **V** Middleton Railway; **W** Stockport Bahamas depot, Dinting; **X** Lochty Private Railway; **Y** Chasewater Depot, Railway Preservation Society.

SECR 0–6–0 tank and an 1885 Adams LSWR 4–4–2 tank, which had many years service on the East Kent Light Railway, although for the last 15 years had been back on former LSWR territory on the Lyme Regis branch. Four Metropolitan Railway coaches of 1900 vintage were also acquired, enabling some 91,000 passengers to be carried in 1961. Since then further arrivals have included GWR No 3217, a "Dukedog" double-framed 4–4–0, a North London Railway 0–6–0 tank of 1880, another "Terrier", No 72 *Fenchurch*, built in 1872 and oldest of its class, LBSC 0–6–2 tank No 473 *Birch Grove* of 1898, and more recently BR Class 4 4–6–0 No 75027. There are also two industrial locomotives, one, an Aveling Porter "steamroller" type, being of particular interest. Other carriages purchased include a former LNWR Observation Saloon used in North Wales, the LBSC Directors Saloon, a Caledonian Railway corridor third, one of the once familiar SECR birdcage roof brakes and several SECR non-corridor thirds.

Altogether, therefore, there is a formidable array of vintage rolling stock assembled at Sheffield Park, where, too, a large collection of old enamelled advertisements can be seen to add to the Victorian atmosphere. Each season there are special attractions such as a veteran motor car week-end, when the staff are suitably attired in period costume. Apart from the delightful scenery, at its best in the spring with an abundance of bluebells and primroses beside the line, there is the added attraction of the National Trust's Sheffield Park Gardens not far from the station.

Another candidate for preservation in the South East is the Kent & East Sussex Railway, of which the 13½ mile section from Robertsbridge to Tenterden survives. Opened in 1902, it was one of a group of light railways run by the late Colonel H. F. Stephens. Taken over by BR in 1948, the passenger service was withdrawn in 1954 and freight traffic ceased seven years later. It was a delightful line through attractive countryside but as a preservation prospect has been beset with difficulties. It crosses some marshland and has in the past been flooded, necessitating increased track maintenance. Its several bridges will only carry locomotives of light axleload and there are no fewer than eight level crossings, of which four are over main trunk roads. Despite hard work on

ABOVE: A heavy train on the Bluebell Railway headed by LSW Adams 4–4–2T No 488, and LBSCR Terrier 0–6–0T *Stepney* seen here near Freshfield on August 8, 1965.   [D. Hill

ABOVE RIGHT: A special train on the Romney Hythe & Dymchurch Railway on June 15, 1968. Driver George Barlow, operating manager of the RHDR, gives engine No 1 *Green Goddess* a final look over before leaving Hythe.
[G. S. Cocks

LEFT: LBSCR Class E4 0–6–2T No 473 *Birch Grove*, one of the Bluebell Railway's larger tank locomotives.   [R. A. Panting

BELOW LEFT: View from inside the Bluebell Railway LNW observation saloon of the line's North London 0–6–0T No 2650 as it approaches Horsted Keynes.
[B. J. Ashworth

track and stations by Preservation Society members, installation of a replacement telephone system throughout the line and the assembly of a large quantity of locomotives and rolling stock, the future looks uncertain since application for a Light Railway Order has been turned down. Nevertheless, the Southern Region has agreed not to lift the track and society work on the line continues unchecked, pending the outcome of further approaches to the Ministry of Transport.

Meanwhile there is much to be seen by visitors and the Preservation Society needs all the support it can muster. Most of the line's rolling stock is kept at Rolvenden. Motive power includes two " Terriers ", one of which, No 70 *Poplar* of 1872, was bought in 1901 by the Rother Valley Railway, predecessor of the KESR. There are also two USA wartime-built 0–6–0 tanks bought by the SR in 1946 for use in Southampton Docks. If the KESR gets going again these powerful engines can be used up the bank from Rolvenden to Tenterden. There are several industrial locomotives, a vintage diesel-electric locomotive, a GWR diesel railcar, several coaches and two Pullman cars. In Colonel Stephens' days there was a wooden shed at Rolvenden and in the yard would stand engines in various stages of decrepitude and decay. Sometimes they were rebuilt; more often they rusted away and were cut up on the spot. Today all the

engines stand in the open but they are well looked after and even if some of the former character of the line is absent there is still plenty of variety.

Also in Kent but in a different category to those already described is the delightful 15in gauge line across Romney Marsh, the Romney, Hythe & Dymchurch Railway. Its claim to be the smallest public railway in the world is founded on fact for it was the subject of a 1926 Light Railway Order and was built to fulfil a public need, since transport facilities in the area were then quite inadequate while holiday traffic was constantly increasing. To be a racing motorist in pre-war days one needed also to be a wealthy man and it was two such gentlemen who subsidised the building of the RH&DR. One, Count Zborowski, was killed in a racing accident before the line opened, but his partner, Captain Howey, retained his interest in the line until his death in 1963. The present double track section from Hythe to New Romney, eight miles in length, opened in 1927, and a five mile extension to Dungeness was completed two years later. This latter stretch was built as double track but reduced to single after the 1939–45 war, during which the line was taken over by the military authorities when among other functions it ran a fully armoured train forming part of the coastal anti-aircraft defence! The line reopened in 1946 with services all the year round as before. The

winter service ceased in 1948 and three years later goods traffic was withdrawn.

The line now operates during the summer months only and it offers a high degree of comfort in its well designed bogie coaches. Its nine locomotives are built to one-third scale proportions in relation to the track gauge, which is of course nearer to one-quarter of the standard gauge size. Five of the engines are based on LNER Gresley A3 Pacifics, *Green Goddess*, *Northern Chief*, *Southern Maid*, *Typhoon*, and *Hurricane*, built between 1925–27, two are free-lance 4–8–2s *Hercules* and *Samson* of 1927, while 1931-built *Winston Churchill* and *Doctor Syn* are 4–6–2s based on Canadian Pacific Railway types.

The main terminus at Hythe has four platform roads and an overall roof, a feature it shares with the stations at Dymchurch and New Romney. The latter place boasts a well-equipped workshop where major overhauls of the locomotives are carried out. Open coaches are in the minority—there are only 16, while there are 12 semi-open, 33 saloon coaches and eight Pullmans. The locomotives are in various liveries and most are equipped with quite melodious chime whistles, which are well in evidence at the numerous level crossings; coaches are now in green and cream livery. The RH&DR has twice changed hands since Captain Howey's death. It remains privately owned and is always well worth a visit to see its immaculate engines and trains. Its popularity continues unabated and passenger traffic in 1968 is reported to have exceeded 320,000, a remarkable figure for a 15in gauge line.

Before leaving Kent, mention should be made of the engines privately preserved at Ashford; they can be visited only on advertised open days. Three are of SECR origin, a rebuilt Stirling 0–6–0 of 1896, a Wainwright 0–6–0 of 1902 and one of the same designer's 0–4–4Ts of 1905. All will eventually be restored to the full glory of the pre-1914 SECR livery. Odd man out here is the LMS Stanier 4–6–0 No 45110 named *RAF Biggin Hill* by the aviators who bought it from BR. The name had already been carried by one of the SR Battle of Britain class engines.

Nearer London, in Surrey, just off the A.25 road between Dorking and Reigate is the Brockham Narrow Gauge Railway Museum. The site is that

ABOVE: Ravenglass & Eskdale 0–8–2 *River Irt* approaches
Irton Road with a train from Dalegarth to Ravenglass on
May 26, 1968. [Allan Stewart

ABOVE: Sunset over GW 0–4–2T No 1466 and its auto-coach, photographed at the GW Society open day on the Cholsey-Wallingford branch on September 21, 1968.
[D. Huntriss

of a disused limestone quarry and some of the track came from nearby Betchworth, whence also came some of the locomotive exhibits. First to arrive, in 1962, was *Townsend Hook* of 3ft 2¼in gauge, built by Fletcher Jennings of Whitehaven in 1880, which worked at Betchworth until 1952. Largest engine at Brockham is the 3ft gauge 0–6–0ST *Scaldwell*, built by Peckett in 1913, from a Northamptonshire ironstone quarry. Other interesting engines include two 2ft gauge Bagnalls, 2–4–0T *Polar Bear*, one of two of its kind which worked the Groudle Glen Railway in the Isle of Man until 1962, and *Peter*, an 0–4–0ST of 1917 built for war service, but latterly used at a Leicestershire quarry. Most unusual exhibit is one of several engines built for the 1ft 10in gauge railway of Messrs Guinness brewery at Dublin. These little engines could be lifted into a 5ft 3in gauge converter truck which they then powered to run on the Irish standard gauge tracks into the brewery. The Brockham Museum houses one of these converter trucks, so telling the whole story of this unique type of engine. In addition to these five steam engines there are seven petrol or diesel engines. Brockham Museum is not normally open to the public and visits can only be made subject to special prior arrangement.

Further west, into Hampshire, is Longmoor, home of the Transportation Training Centre of the Royal Corps of Transport. Construction of a standard gauge line here began in 1905 and the five miles from Bordon to Longmoor were completed two years later. A 3½ mile extension to Liss was opened in 1933. This first came into the field of preservation in 1950 when two engines were restored and exhibited beside the barrack square. One is the smallest standard gauge engine ever built, the 0–4–2T *Gazelle* of 1893 by Dodman of

Kings Lynn, which worked for many years on the Shropshire & Montgomeryshire Light Railway, taken over by the War Department in 1941. The second engine is an Avonside 0–6–0ST *Woolmer*, of 1910 vintage. In 1967 when electrification of the Bournemouth line was completed and steam ceased on the Southern Region, a home was urgently needed for three preserved engines, unrebuilt Bulleid Pacific No 34023 *Blackmore Vale*, the rebuilt No 35029 *Clan Line*, and an Ivatt 2–6–2T No 41298. After negotiations with the army authorities the Association of Railway Preservation Societies found a home for them at Longmoor, where they are only on public view on official open days. Since then they have been joined by David Shepherd's 2–10–0 No 92203 *Black Prince* and 4–6–0 No 75029, also WD 0–6–0ST *Brussels* and a small Andrew Barclay 0–4–0ST of 1915.

In the South West are two lines of note, one of which, the Dart Valley, is described in Chapter 10. The second is a 1ft 6in gauge line, which runs for nearly a mile through the delightful setting of Bicton Gardens, near Budleigh Salterton, Devon. The gardens are worth seeing in themselves for they were planned in the early 18th Century by the French landscape designer responsible for those at Versailles. The railway dates back only to 1963 when the 1916 built Avonside 0–4–0T *Woolwich* arrived. This came from the Royal Arsenal Railway, Woolwich, as did the underframes of some of the coaches. All woodwork had been removed before they left the Arsenal because they had once carried explosives. Now the line boasts three open coaches, two saloons and even a buffet car, and when *Woolwich* is stopped for repairs a diesel engine takes over. The gardens are usually open every afternoon from May to September.

RIGHT: The LBSCR Terrier 0–6–0Ts are well represented among preserved classes. The Kent & East Sussex RPS has acquired *Bodiam* which ran for many years as No 3 on the K&ESR. It is seen here at Rolvenden on February 2, 1969.
[D. A. Idle

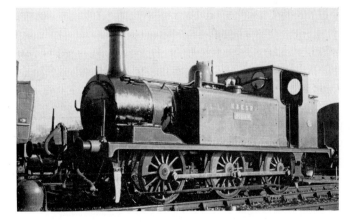

9 Home Counties, Midlands and East Anglia

THE LONDON RPS was established in 1959 as part of the RPS, a national organisation which planned to establish depots where preserved stock could be maintained. Its founder, the late Noel Draycott, wisely thought this of primary importance and that attention could turn to the acquisition of a line later. The three active districts of the RPS are now autonomous societies, although they maintain their close links with each other by membership of the Association of Railway Preservation Societies, which exists to co-ordinate the activities of its members.

Until recently the London RPS has maintained its stock on private sidings at Aylesbury, Bishops Stortford and Luton, but apart from the fact that they were scattered these had the disadvantage of not being normally accessible to the public. Now negotiations have been concluded for part of the site of Quainton Road station, near Aylesbury, on the GCR London Extension. Here will be established a railway preservation centre using the former Brill branch platform and sidings to house nearly 20 engines and some coaches. It is hoped to erect covered accommodation to house much of the collection. Among the large relics are a Metropolitan Railway 0–4–4T, one of the famous LSWR Beattie 2–4–0Ts of 1874, which worked the Wenford mineral branch in North Cornwall until 1962, and one of the diminutive NER inside

cylinder 0–4–0Ts, latterly used at a Nottinghamshire colliery. Rolling stock items include an LNW 12-wheeled kitchen diner of 1901 and 19th century non-bogie coaches of GNR and LCDR origin. The society or its members own a dozen or so engines of industrial type including an Aveling Porter four-coupled gearless engine of 1895, a veteran Hunslet 0–4–0ST of 1882 and the last Kerr Stuart built engine, a 90hp 0–4–0 diesel, still unfinished when the Stoke works closed in 1930 and completed at Hunslet's works, Leeds.

The other RPS English district, as the pioneer group of the organisation, has now taken the title of "The Railway Preservation Society", formerly having been known as the West Midlands RPS. The RPS has a depot beside the LNWR Walsall–Rugeley line at Hednesford, which houses the last surviving LBSC Stroudley E1 0–6–0T of 1877, larger than the same designer's famous "Terriers", this engine having been used at a local colliery from 1926 to 1963. Coaching stock includes a Maryport & Carlisle Railway six-wheeler of 1879, a GER brake of 1885, an LNWR Travelling Post Office vehicle of 1909 and a Midland Railway Royal Saloon of 1912. These can be seen on the regular open days but are not accessible to the public at other times.

Another RPS venture nearing fruition is the operation of a short length of line beside Chase-

ABOVE: One of the Railway Preservation Society's 0–4–0STs and an interesting collection of passenger brake vans and freight stock at the RPS Chasewater depot, photographed in September 1968. [G. Wildish

LEFT: The general manager of the Cadeby Light Railway, the Rev. Teddy Boston, drives Bagnall 0–4–0ST *Pixie* on the 100yd long Cadeby Light Railway, situated in the grounds of Cadeby Rectory. [R. C. Riley

water Pool, a local beauty spot and important recreational centre in the Cannock Chase area. Part of the line, about a mile beyond Brownhills station is all that is left of the MR Brownhills branch opened from Aldridge in 1882 and closed to passengers in 1930. The colliery extension opened two years later but traffic continued until 1960, when most of the line was lifted. The RPS line remaining links up with a line leased from the NCB, once part of 11 miles of mineral railways authorised in 1866 as the Cannock Chase & Wolverhampton Railway. The Wolverhampton extension was never built. When a considerable amount of track relaying has been done and the RPS gets going these lines will carry their first passengers. All the locomotives at Chasewater are of industrial types, four or six-coupled engines most suitable for running on lightly-laid track. The steam fleet includes an Andrew Barclay fireless locomotive of 1917, an unusual and interesting engine of a type charged with steam from a stationary boiler. Engines of this type were much favoured in factory sidings where smoke or sparks could not be permitted. Oldest member of the fleet is a Neilson saddle tank of 1882 from Gartsherrie Iron Works near Glasgow. As soon as covered accommodation is available in the extensive storage compound the rolling stock from Hednesford will be transferred to Chasewater and once track relaying is complete the RPS will be in business.

Another Staffordshire line is already running in the summer months. This is the Foxfield Railway which operates two four-coupled industrial saddle tanks over the four miles of track connecting the Derby–Crewe line with the former Foxfield Colliery at Dilhorne, about five miles from Stoke-on-Trent. This line is open on one Sunday each month and at other times by prior arrangement. One LMS passenger coach is available but as a rule suitably adapted goods vehicles are used.

Not in steam, alas, but worth a visit are the railway relics housed in the Staffordshire County Museum at Shugborough Hall, near Stafford. These include a North Stafford 0–6–2T built at Stoke in 1923, a battery-electric locomotive of the same company, an LNWR Ramsbottom 0–4–0ST of 1865, and one of the attractive little red saddle tanks once familiar on the extensive Bass brewery system at Burton-on-Trent.

A rather offbeat line is to be found near Market Bosworth. In fact it is the Cadeby Light Railway, which runs in the grounds of Cadeby Rectory right beside the A447 road, five miles north of Hinckley. In the old days it is said that steam engines when they had occasion to run in the streets would startle horses unaccustomed to the sight, often with unfortunate results. Nowadays the unexpected whistle of the 1919 Bagnall *Pixie* as it steams round this garden in the heart of the Leicestershire countryside has caused amazement among passing motorists unprepared for the sight, though happily without dire consequences. The railway runs on the second Saturday of each month during the summer or at other times by special arrangement with the General Manager, who is none other than the Rev. E. R. Boston, incumbent of the parish. Never on Sundays, though, but Teddy Boston will always be happy to welcome you then at either Cadeby or Sutton Cheney churches, when you can be sure of attending a simple service taken with dignity and sincerity in a delightful setting. *Pixie* is a 2ft gauge engine from an ironstone line—there are other steam engines in various stages of dismantling, and some diesels. You are almost certain to see a traction engine in steam, too, and an annual rally is held nearby. The extensive model railway system must not be missed. In 1970 it is hoped to have another short line operating in the vicinity—at Church Farm, Newbold Verdon, with *Pamela* and *Sybil Mary*, a pair of 1906 Hunslets from Penrhyn Quarries, North Wales.

Near Tyseley station, just south of Birmingham is a large BR diesel depot, until recent years an important Western Region steam shed. In the summer of 1968 the former coaling stage and its approach tracks were leased by Clun Castle Ltd a company established by leading railway preservationist P. B. Whitehouse, who was previously associated with the Talyllyn Railway and who is now chairman of the Dart Valley Railway; this

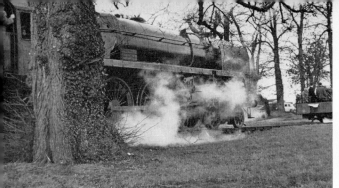

TOP LEFT: BR Britannia Pacific No 70013 *Oliver Cromwell* is now housed at Bressingham Hall, Diss, where it is steamed occasionally on a short length of track.

[B. Lowe

TOP RIGHT: LMS Jubilee 4–6–0 No 5593 *Kolhapur* is steamed occasionally at its Tyseley depot home on special open days.

[V. C. K. Allen

BELOW: LMS Princess Royal Pacific No 46201 *Princess Elizabeth* is preserved in company with two LMS coaches by the Dowty Railway Preservation Society at Ashchurch.

[Princess Elizabeth Locomotive Society

part of the depot has been converted to accommodate WR Castle 4–6–0 No 7029 *Clun Castle*, in GW livery although built by BR in 1950, and LMS Jubilee 4–6–0 No 5593 *Kolhapur*, of 1934 carefully restored in LMS livery. These engines are to be seen on regular open days, or by special arrangement at other times. Both are in good condition and it is to be hoped that in due course they may again be permitted to haul special trains on BR tracks. Also here is Stanier Class 5 4–6–0 No 5428, recently restored to LMS livery and now named *Eric Treacy* after the Bishop of Wakefield, well known as a railway enthusiast.

The occupational hazards of preserving a large steam locomotive had already been learnt the hard way by the few stalwarts of the Princess Elizabeth Locomotive Society who acquired the famous 1933 LMS Pacific No 6201 *Princess Elizabeth* in 1963. Buying such a machine—weighing 160 tons in working order—is one thing but maintaining it in good condition when stored in the open is quite another. After two years of hard work came the

great day when it was steamed again—fortunately a thrush that had nested under the footplate had raised its brood and flown away! Much had been done, but alas, when water was put in the boiler for the first time leaks were so bad that it had to be emptied causing flooding of the track, which sagged under the weight. Roger Bell, indefatigable Society secretary, managed to fit new asbestos gaskets and in the process everything was damped but his enthusiasm! It was all right on the day although there were anxious moments when it was found easy to move the engine on a short siding, less easy to stop it. Much has been learnt from those early lessons and in 1967 and 1968 *Princess Elizabeth* steamed from its Ashchurch home at the invitation of BR to be present at the open days at Bristol Bath Road depot. The Society also has two LMS coaches and a six-wheeled full brake of the 1930s, the latter vehicle beautifully restored. *Princess Elizabeth* should be fully restored to LMS livery by the end of 1969.

The Ashchurch site mentioned is part of a unique

preservation venture, for it occupies part of the private sidings at one of the works of the Dowty Group. This enlightened firm runs an active Sports and Social Club and so railway preservation becomes one section, on a par with cricket, tennis and so on. The Dowty RPS owns some interesting GWR vehicles, mentioned in Chapter 10, also an Avonside four-coupled tank donated by Cadbury Bros. from their Bournville factory, among many smaller and no less interesting relics. *George B*, an 1898 Hunslet narrow-gauge saddle tank, one of many Dinorwic slate quarries' engines to be preserved, is in steam on open days held during the year, but there is no public access at other times.

In East Anglia the longest standing preservation venture is that of the M&GN Joint Railway Society, which set out in 1959 to preserve the line from North Walsham Town to Yarmouth Beach. This ambitious scheme came to nothing and thoughts then turned to the Melton Constable—Norwich City line. This, too, did not materialise and present plans are concerned with the two miles of line from Sheringham to Weybourne. The Society now uses both these Norfolk stations and at the former houses a Great Eastern Railway 0–6–0 of 1912 and an LNER-built Class B12 4–6–0, a Gresley rebuild of a GER design, both the last survivors of their classes. There are also two BR diesel railbuses, a four-coach set of Gresley articulated suburban coaches, and a GER coach. The 0–6–0 has been steamed, but now requires retubing, as does the 4–6–0, which draws attention to the unfortunate effects of deterioration caused by open storage, an unpleasant fact that has to be faced by all preservation societies lacking adequate covered storage accommodation.

The delightful gardens of Bressingham Hall, near Diss in Norfolk, cover more than 400 acres and have been open to the public on Thursday and Sunday afternoons each summer for many years. Steam power has been represented for some years, too, for there is an interesting and varied collection of traction engines, rollers, ploughing engines, portables, steam wagons and a showman's engine. In 1964 a 9½in gauge line with free-lance 4–6–2 and open trucks was obtained from Danson Park, Welling. Two years later a 2ft gauge line was laid which enables visitors to see the nursery gardens, not otherwise open to the public. Motive power is provided by Hunslet 0–4–0 tanks *Gwynedd* (1883) and *George Sholto* (1909), quarry engines from Penrhyn, both owned by Alan Bloom, while privately preserved *Maid Marian* (1903) from Dinorwic, is also to be seen. In 1967 an even

larger engine arrived, a 3ft 3in gauge Peckett 0–6–0ST from an ironstone line at Wellingborough Northants.

Meanwhile, Alan Bloom, the owner of Bressingham Hall, was still hankering after the real thing—something of 12in to the foot scale. The first standard gauge engine to arrive was a diminutive four-coupled saddle tank once used in the retort houses of Beckton Gasworks, East London, preserved by the Industrial Locomotive Society. In contrast, another industrial engine came from the NCB after many years at Atherstone Colliery, near Tamworth, Staffordshire, *William Francis*, a large 0–4–0+0–4–0 Garratt built by Beyer Peacock in 1927. This requires much attention before it can be steamed and it will be restored to its original blue livery, the last standard-gauge survivor of its type in the country. The remaining three engines have been loaned by BR; foremost among these is Britannia Pacific No 70013 *Oliver Cromwell*, built in 1952, the last steam engine overhauled in BR workshops, which hauled BR's last steam special on August 11, 1968. A few days later it was at Diss, to which it was no stranger, for it spent the first 10 years of its life at Norwich depot working expresses to and from London. The other engines at Bressingham are the London Tilbury & Southend Railway 4–4–2T *Thundersley* of 1909, restored to its old livery although not in its original condition—perhaps one can condone a degree of artistic licence occasionally, to see the splendour of the pre-grouping railway's colours—and its successor of LMS days, the first Stanier three-cylinder 2–6–4T No 2500 of 1934, which spent most of its life on the LTS line. There have been steam open days on the first Sunday of each month during the winter, when *Oliver Cromwell* has steamed up and down the sharp gradient leading to the drive from the museum building in which it is housed. As soon as they are in a fit state it is hoped to steam the other standard gauge engines from time to time.

A short narrow-gauge line is to be found at Humberston, near Grimsby. The Lincolnshire Coast Light Railway commenced operations in 1960 with a Peckett 0–6–0ST *Jurassic* of 1903, from the Rugby Portland Cement Co's Southam works. The track and coaching stock are of first world war origin and two of the three coaches saw service on the Ashover Light Railway. The 1899 Hunslet 0–4–0ST *Elin* from Penrhyn is a more recent arrival, while three vintage diesels are also available. The line operates daily during the summer months.

10 *The Great Western preserved*

OF ALL the large British railway companies one has always seemed to stand head and shoulders above the rest as a shrine for railway enthusiasm—the Great Western. Its dedicated adherents are so many and so active that there are more GWR engines and items of rolling stock preserved than those of any other company. Leading present day enthusiasm is the Great Western Society and its record of preservation is impressive. Its main collection is housed in the former engine shed at Didcot, by arrangement with BR Western Region, but it is not at present open to the public. However, open days are regularly arranged on the nearby branch line from Cholsey to Wallingford and on these occasions one of the once familiar 0–4–2 tanks and railmotor trailers usually conveys passengers to and fro, while another engine is on show in steam. The 0–4–2 tank, No 1466, and its coach have been beautifully restored to GWR livery and work is progressing on other preserved engines at Didcot which include 4–6–0 No 6998 *Burton Agnes Hall*, 2–6–2 tank No 6106, and Alexandra Docks' Railway 0–4–0ST No 1340 *Trojan*, the latter preserved by an independent society which also owns Cardiff Railway 0–4–0ST No 1338 kept at Bleadon, near Weston-super-Mare. Recent acquisitions are diesel railcar No 4, built in 1934 and loaned by BR, Churchward Mogul

No 5322 (at Caerphilly) and the 1857 0–4–0T Wantage Tramway No 5. Also at Didcot is privately owned Castle class 4–6–0 No 4079 *Pendennis Castle*, which is not likely to emerge until BR relaxes its intransigent attitude to steam-worked excursions on its tracks. GW carriages at Didcot include one of the 1932 Plymouth Ocean Liner saloons and the last survivor of the 1905 Dreadnought stock.

Two other Great Western Society engines are looked after by the Dowty Preservation Society at Ashchurch. These are 4–6–0 No 7808 *Cookham Manor* and 0–6–2T No 6697, both of which have been steamed from time to time. The Ashchurch site has been mentioned in Chapter 9 and its relics are not confined to those of the GWR. However, it also houses the only surviving coach of the GWR 1935 centenary stock, a restaurant car, and it has a rather splendid GWR saloon of 1881 vintage. There are many smaller relics of the Great Western to be seen on the regular open days. In 1968 *Cookham Manor* ran in steam to BR's open days at Bristol and Tyseley. At the latter depot, in the suburbs of Birmingham, privately owned 4–6–0 No 7029 *Clun Castle* is housed and was also steamed on the same occasion.

Thirty miles from Birmingham is the interesting old market town of Bridgnorth where the River

LEFT: The Dart Valley Railway reopened at Easter 1969, although only between Totnes and Buckfastleigh. Most trains will be formed of WR saloon push-pull trailers and the heavier trains will be worked by 2–6–2T No 4555 seen here on a trial run at Ashburton.

RIGHT: The GW Society organises occasional open days in conjunction with British Railways on the Cholsey-Wallingford branch; on some occasions the Society's GW 0–4–2T No 1466 may be seen in steam. It is seen here on April 15, 1968 with the Society's push and pull saloon coach.   [D. B. Clark.

Severn divides the town in two. A remarkable feature here is the Castle Hill Railway dating from 1892, the only inland cliff railway in the country, built to connect the riverside with High Town. Another interesting feature is the lengthy 1895 built footbridge which connects High Town with the station, where one can see the activities of the Severn Valley Railway Society. The Severn Valley Railway was opened in 1862 and linked Shrewsbury and Worcester. The SVR was 41 miles in length and at the southern end it joined the Wolverhampton–Worcester line at Hartlebury, 11 miles north of Worcester. In latter years passenger traffic dwindled and was finally withdrawn in 1963, when, too, the section from Buildwas to Alveley was closed to all traffic. Two years later the SVRS was formed to preserve the five mile stretch from Bridgnorth to Hampton Loade. Until recently the southern end of the line as far as Alveley, just south of Hampton Loade, was used for BR coal traffic and formed a ready means of access for SVRS rolling stock. Since it was formed rather late in the day to acquire GW locomotives in good condition, several of its locomotives are of LMS design, 2–8–0 No 48773, which saw wartime service in Persia, 2–6–0s Nos 43106 and 46443 and 0–6–0T No 47383. The GW is represented by 0–6–0 No 3205, built in 1946 and a Port Talbot Railway 0–6–0ST of 1901. There are also two industrial locomotives, one of which was the last engine to be built by the famous firm of Manning Wardle of Leeds, in 1926. Recently restored to GWR livery is diesel railcar No 22, built in 1941, a type of vehicle often used on the line in GW days; there is a formidable collection of rolling stock, mostly of GW origin, including a Plymouth ocean liner saloon, two of the 1921-built low-roof coaches used on the London suburban services that traversed the Metropolitan Railway, corridor coaches of the 1920s and 1930s, a 1930-built railmotor trailer, a Dean 40ft parcels van of the 1890s and a milk train brake van. A useful purchase in 1968 was the Stourbridge breakdown train, a steam crane and accompanying tool vans. SVRS members have shown considerable energy in restoring their track and rolling stock and although the line does not yet operate regularly it is to be hoped that the SVRPS will be granted their light railway order to work the line which runs through beautiful countryside with fine views of the River Severn. Meanwhile Bridgnorth station is open to the public and there is a great deal to see.

One of the most famous GWR locomotives ever is to be found in a most unlikely place some miles south west of Bridgnorth, for BR has recently allowed 4–6–0 No 6000 *King George V* to go on extended loan to Messrs H. P. Bulmer Ltd at its Hereford cider factory. Here, too, are five Pullman coaches forming an exhibition train. Members of the local group of the Great Western Society have volunteered to keep *King George V* in first class condition, following its overhaul and restoration to BR livery by a firm at Newport. Regular open days are held at Hereford, when the engine can be seen. Tickets issued on such occasions bear the wording " Issued subject to the Conditions and Regulations of the Bulmers Railways Board's Publications and Notices wherein you are henceforth constrained to consume at least one glass of Bulmers Cider per day." The rumour that *King George V*'s tender contains 4,000 gallons of cider can be emphatically denied!

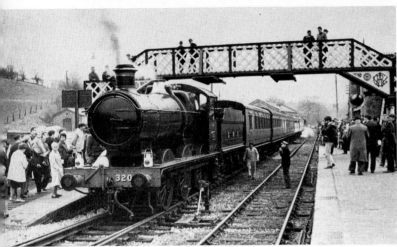

ABOVE: Other Great Western preserved steam locomotives have been seen
on public display at occasional open days
at Bristol Bath Road diesel depot. The
two engines here are Manor class 4–6–0
No 7808 *Cookham Manor* and 0–6–2T
No 6697. [Ivo Peters

LEFT: The Severn Valley Railway Preservation Society is hoping to reopen the
section between Bridgnorth and Hampton Loade and has already acquired a
selection of LMS and GW locomotives
and stock. GW 0–6–0 No 3205 is seen at
Bridgnorth on one of the Society open
days. [P. Kingston

Probably many people came to know and love
the Great Western in the course of holiday journeys,
especially on its many attractive branch lines. It is
particularly appropriate that a branch in the West
Country has been saved, the Dart Valley line from
Totnes to Ashburton in Devon. Opened in 1872
the line is 9½ miles in length, but passenger trains
ceased in 1958 and the goods service was withdrawn four years later. Since then negotiations
have been taking place with a view to purchase of
the line to run a train service as an attraction to the
many thousands of holidaymakers in the area.
These efforts so far have met with difficulty because
the Ministry of Transport envisages the use of part
of the trackbed between Ashburton and Buckfastleigh for improvements to the A38 trunk road.
Since the economic situation necessitates a very
low priority for this particular road expenditure,
there is hope that the Dart Valley line may open
throughout for a few years even if eventually it
may have to be truncated. Scenically the line has a

great deal to commend it especially on the 7 miles
between Totnes and Buckfastleigh reopened for
passenger service at Easter 1969.

Already at Buckfastleigh there are nine GWR
engines and twice that number of carriages. Most
of the engines are traditional branch line engines,
such as the 1924 built 2–6–2T No 4555, the two
0–4–2T motor train engines and the three similar
0–6–0 pannier tanks. Another pannier tank,
No 1638, is one of a type built at Swindon in BR
days to replace older small engines; built as
recently as 1951 it was soon replaced by the ever
encroaching diesel. Odd man out at Buckfastleigh
is a small but powerful pannier tank, No 1369,
built in 1934, one of a type used on lines where a
short wheelbase was necessary, such as the tramway
line to Weymouth Quay. More of a shunting
engine than a branch engine, nevertheless it should
be recalled that these diminutive machines used to
take charge of Channel Islands boat trains along
the quayside lines at Weymouth. There are some

RIGHT UPPER: Among the larger loco-motives now privately owned is GW 4–6–0 No 4079 *Pendennis Castle* normally housed at Didcot. Because of the BRB ban on steam working there is at present no prospect of this engine being used on BR metals. [P. Hocquard]

RIGHT LOWER: Another large Great Western engine now preserved is King class 4–6–0 No 6000 *King George V*; although on the official BR list it is on loan to Bulmers of Hereford where it is looked after by the local branch of the GW Society. The engine has been over-hauled and is in working order. [J. C. Sawtell]

interesting coaches, too, apart from the workaday railmotor trailers and corridor coaches used on daily trains for three Pullman cars, one of which was observation car on the " Devon Belle " and two of the equally luxurious GWR ocean liner saloons are on the branch. Four older coaches retain the old fashioned clerestory roof, two Dean engineer's saloons of the 1890s, the Churchward dynamometer car of 1901 and a Churchward engineer's saloon of 1910 vintage. Most of these carriages have been smartly repainted in the old GWR chocolate and cream livery, while the engines, too, are in the well remembered green.

Before leaving the Great Western some other isolated engines call for comments: one is a six-coupled saddle tank of 1910 built for Plymouth Docks shunting and now looked after by the South Western group of the GW Society. Its future is obscure but there is a possible home for it in the former engine shed at Bodmin, Cornwall. Also homeless at present is the only surviving Church-

ward 2–8–0, No 2818, built in 1905. This is eventually to find a home in a museum at Bristol, but regrettably it will never steam again. The Bluebell Line has already been mentioned and there one can occasionally see at work No 3217 *Earl of Berkeley*, an outside framed " Dukedog " 4–4–0, a type once familiar on the Cambrian system and on branch lines not suitable for larger engines. The only survivor of the GWR broad-gauge era is a curious little four-coupled vertical boiler engine to be seen on the down platform at Newton Abbot station, the South Devon Railway *Tiny* of 1868.

Swindon Museum houses Churchward 4–6–0 No 4003 *Lode Star* of 1907, the famous 4–4–0 *City of Truro*, said to have attained 102.3mph in 1904, a Dean Goods 0–6–0 of 1897, 0–6–0PT No 9400, prototype of the last GWR built 0–6–0 pannier tank and the replica *North Star*, together with many interesting smaller relics. A Taff Vale 0–6–2T is undergoing restoration at Caerphilly, where also 2–6–0 No 5322 is housed.

11   *The North*

A LINE with gradients of 1 in 30 and curves of 3½ chains radius in an industrial part of Leeds sounds an unpromising prospect but such was the first standard gauge line to be preserved in this country. The Middleton Railway proudly claims ancestry back to 1758 when parliamentary authority was given for the laying down of a " waggonway " for the carriage of coals. Steam traction was introduced to the line as early as 1812, more than a decade before Stephenson's *Rocket* was built. After nationalisation of the coal industry in 1947 the NCB leased the line, decided that it worked at a loss and ceased to operate it, thereby leaving a number of firms with rail access but no trains. In 1959 a number of Leeds University enthusiasts decided to rectify this state of affairs and after much attention to the permanent way a portion of the line serving two works was reopened in the summer of 1960 and a regular freight service now operates, exchanging traffic with BR to the extent of about 10,000 tons a year. The line is operated entirely by volunteers and a very creditable job they are doing. Indeed it is the only freight line operated as a preservation-style venture.

Recently the opportunity has arisen to purchase from the NCB the line to Middleton Colliery and to rent some of the buildings at the pit-head, which is the most historic part of the line still in being. At present the engines are kept in the open and the buildings would provide the much needed maintenance depot and museum. The 1758 Middleton Railway Trust has launched an appeal for the required funds and this is indeed a worthy cause that deserves to succeed.

The Middleton line has to be seen to be believed and is quite unlike any other preserved line anywhere. Even if its daily job is less glamorous than that of some of the other lines it is well worthwhile and is carried on efficiently and without fuss. First engine on the line was a 150hp 1932 vintage diesel bought in 1960 from its makers, the Hunslet Engine Co.; this has been named *John Alcock* after the Managing Director of the firm at that time. There are two other diesels, a diminutive 22hp Hunslet that has been well cared for at Courage's Alton Brewery, and another product of Leeds, a Fowler-built machine. Most attractive steam engine to be seen is a Gateshead-built NER four-coupled side tank of 1891 well restored to original livery and preserved in 1965 by the Steam Power Trust. Another four-coupled engine which saw service on the LNER is one of the once-familiar vertical boiler Sentinel steam engines, built in 1933. There are also some four and six-coupled industrial steam engines, some goods vehicles including a Midland Railway goods brake van, and a steam crane. Open days are held on the Middleton line at regular intervals when the immaculate NER tank and one of the other engines are usually in steam. At the Steam Gala in 1968 in addition to the usual attractions there were eight steam road engines on parade and no fewer than three fairground steam organs providing powerful background music!

Not far north of Leeds is the town of Haworth, made famous as a tourist centre by the 19th century writings of the Brontë sisters. With the 1968 reopening of the Worth Valley branch line by the Keighley & Worth Valley Railway Preservation

LEFT: A general view of Haworth yard on the Keighley & Worth Valley Railway on August 3, 1968. On the left Ivatt 2–6–2T No 41241 arrives with a train from Oxenhope. [Derek Cross

RIGHT: LMS " Crab " 2–6–0 No 2700 undergoes steaming tests at Oxenhope on September 7, 1968 as one of the KWVR's two four-wheel railbuses arrives from Keighley. [Ian G. Holt

Society, having its headquarters at Haworth, the town now has another claim to fame. The five-mile branch line from Keighley to Oxenhope, one mile beyond Haworth, was opened in 1867 and worked by the Midland Railway. It is a line of severe gradients and indeed climbs all the way to Oxenhope, where the rugged country scenery provides a marked contrast to the urban conurbation of Keighley. After 18 months of working by diesel railcar units BR finally decided that the branch was uneconomic and passenger trains were withdrawn at the end of 1961, goods traffic following six months later. Then began lengthy negotiations with BR by the very active Preservation Society, culminating in the triumphant reopening in June 1968.

Apart from the scenery and the attraction of hearing standard gauge engines working really hard on the gradients, the KWVRPS has assembled the largest collection of engines and coaches of any preserved lines. These include 24 steam engines, a 500hp diesel, two diesel railbuses and about 20 varied examples of coaching stock, many more than can conveniently be described here. Most, if not at work on the line, are to be found in the sidings

at Haworth. Main line engines include Royal Scot 4–6–0 No 46115 (which may move to Dinting), Stanier Class 5 4–6–0 No 45212, LMS No 2700, the pioneer Fowler 2–6–0 loaned by BR, a GNR 0–6–0ST of 1897 and 0–6–2T of 1921, a Midland Railway 0–6–0T of 1880 and 0–6–0 of 1920, four L&Y goods engines, an 0–6–0T of NER design built in BR days, one of the LMS Ivatt 2–6–2Ts, once familiar on the branch, and an 0–6–0T of USA origin once used at Southampton Docks; there are also some industrial engines. Coaching stock is no less interesting, ranging from Pullman Cars and vintage officers inspection saloons to some four and six-wheeled vehicles built between 1870 and 1888 and an LMS non-corridor third of the 1930s. From the south come three Metropolitan Railway coaches and a corridor coach of a type built by the SECR for its continental boat trains in 1922–3, while the Gresley Society has loaned three fine LNER coaches of 1937–9, including one of the beavertail observation cars built for the crack " Coronation " express. Altogether this is a magnificent assembly of large relics of the steam age and there is the added attraction of seeing them at work.

RIGHT: The Middleton Railway is the only one of the preserved lines which carries freight only. Two of the line's locomotives, a Bagnall 0–4–0ST and an NER 0–4–0T, head a train of tank wagons on September 2, 1967. [A. M. Bowman

ABOVE: Ravenglass & Eskdale 2–8–2 *River Mite* heads a crowded passenger train from Eskdale Green to Dalegarth on May 26, 1968.   [Allan Stewart
LEFT: Another LMS Jubilee 4–6–0 to be preserved is No 5596 *Bahamas* stabled at Dinting depot.   [Keith Smith
RIGHT: Four other LNER Pacifics besides *Flying Scotsman* have been preserved privately in Great Britain, three of which are A4 streamliners. Top right is No 4498 *Sir Nigel Gresley* in LNER livery which was used on a number of enthusiasts' specials. Below right are Class A4 Pacific No 60019 *Bittern* and Class A2 Pacific No 60532 *Blue Peter*.   A. McBurnie

A prospect not yet realised but which will perform a valuable public service if it succeeds is that of the North Yorkshire Moors RPS, which plans to purchase the 18 mile line from Grosmont to High Mill, Pickering, of which the seven miles from Grosmont has the track in position, while the rest must be relaid. Some of the villages served by this line become snowbound in the winter months, hence the Society has considerable support from local Councils. The Society's present base is at Goathland station, where a diesel railbus and a first class sleeping car provide a mobile base for working parties. If negotiations with BR are successful other Societies have offered suitable motive power. These are likely to include a North Eastern Railway 0–8–0 of 1918 and an 0–6–0 of 1923, and an 0–6–2T of GER design built at Stratford in 1924. The line is outstanding in the beauty of its moorland scenery and once formed part of the Whitby & Pickering Railway, 24 miles

in length, which opened for horse traction as far back as 1836, locomotive haulage being introduced in 1847. BR closed the line in 1965 despite considerable local opposition. Until 1865 the line included a cable-worked incline at Grosmont, but in that year a deviation line was opened with a gradient of 1 in 49. Indeed it is a line of steep gradients throughout on which locomotives needed to be worked hard, and where one hopes to see them at work again in the future.

Right across the country from East to West, the Cumberland coast is reached, where there is a railway survival that is very different. The Ravenglass & Eskdale Railway started life in 1875 as a 3ft gauge line for the conveyance of iron ore traffic and it survived in this form until 1912, when the mines closed after being progressively run down. In addition to the mineral traffic the line had carried passengers since 1876. Had it not been for the interest of Mr W. J. Bassett-Lowke, the famous

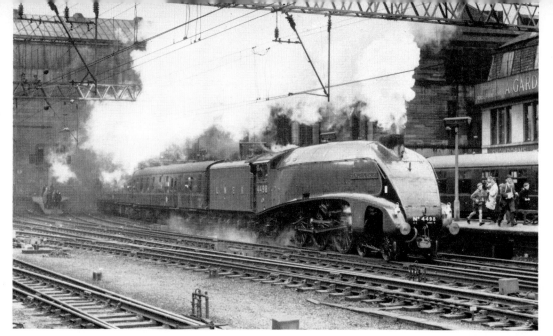

miniature railway engineer, the R&ER might have ended its days, but instead he realised the value of the line as a testbed for his locomotives and in 1915 work started on its conversion to 15in gauge. Two years later the eight miles of track to the old terminus at Boot had been converted and the line was reopened throughout in its new form. Since the ore mines at Boot had been worked out there was no longer any need for this part of the line, which was in any case very steep for the miniature locomotives. Hence in 1922 the more easily accessible Dalegarth terminus was opened, seven miles from Ravenglass. The line eventually came into the ownership of the Keswick Granite Company, whose quarries provided much traffic for the railway until their closure in 1953. Five years later the line was advertised for sale as a going concern and in 1960 it was sold by auction to the Ravenglass & Eskdale RPS, thanks largely to the financial assistance of the late Colin Gilbert.

The railway was in reasonably good condition and apart from internal combustion engines owned two powerful steam locomotives, 2–8–2 *River Esk* of 1923 and 0–8–2 *River Irt* of 1928. The line traverses pleasant countryside on the fringe of the Lake District, with views of the distant hills. Thanks to extensive publicity and strong support from the Society membership the line's popularity increases each year and in 1968 it carried over 210,000 passengers compared with only 37,000 ten years earlier. Another remarkable achievement was in December 1966 when the railway took delivery of a brand new steam locomotive, the 2–8–2 *River Mite*. Built at York, its cost has been raised by loans and donations from Society members and the public alike. It was transported to Ravenglass over the Pennines in appalling weather conditions behind a steam traction engine. Having overcome initial teething troubles *River Mite* has settled down to being a useful member of the R&ER stud and for engines in immaculate condition these three take a lot of beating. The railway has 27 open coaches and since 1965 it has been steadily increasing its stock of closed saloon coaches, which now number eight vehicles. Only a small proportion of the old freight stock survives for use on works trains.

Also in the Lake District, preservation activities are well under way on the former Furness Railway line from Ulverston to Lakeside, completed in 1868. The branch, just under eight miles in length joins the main Barrow-Carnforth line at Plumpton Junction, 1½ miles from Ulverston. Since the main line still carries BR traffic the Lakeside (Windermere) Railway Society and its parent company can only hope to restore trains to the branch itself. Opposition from the Lake District Planning Board, which planned to convert two miles of the trackbed into a footpath, has at last been overcome. Meanwhile the Lakeside Company has leased part of the BR motive power depot at Carnforth, where some of its locomotives are housed. These include Ivatt 2–6–0 No 46441 in maroon livery (a distinction it shares with the KWVR Ivatt 2–6–2T), two LMS Fairburn 2–6–4Ts and no fewer than six LMS Stanier Class 5 4–6–0s, including No 44767, the sole example with Stephenson valve gear, which is privately owned. Another interesting acquisition is *Sir Robert* from NCB Walkden, near Manchester, a North Stafford 0–6–2T built at Stoke in 1920. One of the company directors has stored elsewhere a number of industrial type engines, some of which will be made

available for works trains on the line, and these include a North British Railway four coupled " Pug Tank " of 1887. The running of steam trains to the pleasant terminus beside Lake Windermere will add yet another tourist attraction to the Lake District.

At Dinting, near Glossop, Derbyshire, not far from the Lancashire border, a former Great Central Railway engine shed, and its seven acre site, has been acquired as a museum for steam preservation by the Bahamas Locomotive Society. Pride of place among the contents is LMS Jubilee 4–6–0 No 5596 *Bahamas*, which unlike its sisters, apart from two rebuilt with larger boilers, ended its BR days with a double chimney. This engine has been overhauled by the Hunslet Engine Company, Leeds, and restored to LMS maroon livery. The shed also provides a home for a Hudswell Clarke 0–6–0T of 1938, and a vintage diesel. An increase in the amount of covered accommodation is envisaged for the future. Meanwhile there are open days when *Bahamas* can be seen in steam and in view of its good mechanical condition one hopes that eventually it may be seen again on British Railways metals.

The City of Liverpool will eventually exhibit some preserved locomotives which include the last Mersey Railway engine, 0–6–4T *Cecil Raikes* of 1885, Mersey Docks & Harbour Board No 1, an Avonside 0–6–0ST of 1904, together with Liverpool & Manchester Railway 0–4–2 *Lion* of 1838, well remembered for its important part in the film *The Titfield Thunderbolt*.

12 *Scotland*

IN SCOTLAND railway preservation has been no less active than in England and Wales. The Scottish RPS dates back to the founding of the intended national organisation in 1959. It is now an independent society and has achieved much in the last decade. Its assembly of large relics is impressive; they are housed in a former goods shed at Springfield yard, near Falkirk Grahamston station, where they can be seen on open days or at other times by special arrangement.

Pride of the Falkirk Museum collection is Caledonian Railway 0–4–4T No 419, built at St. Rollox in 1907, and withdrawn at the end of 1962. Restoration was no longer possible at St. Rollox and was carried out by the firm next door, the

former North British Railway workshops at Cowlairs. At the same time the engine was overhauled to make it fit to steam if the occasion arises. It is a beautiful sight in its handsome Caley blue livery; the museum is worth visiting just to see No 419, but in fact there is much more. A second main line engine is the North British Railway 0–6–0 *Maude* of 1891. The name, that of an Army General of the first world war, was given to the engine on its return from military service in France, and so it is specially deserving of preservation.

The Scottish RPS has also seven industrial locomotives, of which the oldest is the 0–4–0WT *Ellesmere*, built by Hawthorns of Leith in 1861, while there is a Neilson 0–4–0ST only 15 years

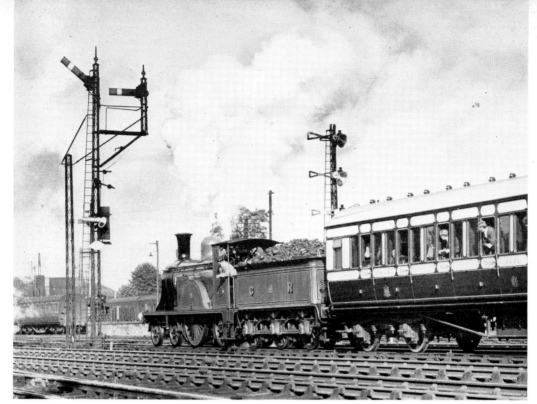

ABOVE: The Scottish Region used a number of preserved Scottish locomotives on enthusiasts' specials before they were finally retired to museums. Caledonian 4–2–2 No 123 is seen leaving Perth on October 11, 1958 with an SLS special. [W. J. V. Anderson

RIGHT: The Scottish Railway Preservation Society has numerous Scottish relics at its Falkirk depot, including Caledonian 0–4–4T No 419 and Caledonian, Great North of Scotland and Highland coaches. [Scottish RPS

BELOW: Most of the preserved Scottish locomotives are housed in Glasgow Transport Museum. Engines in the photograph below include Highland 4–6–0 No 103, NBR 4–4–0 No 256, GNSR 4–4–0 No 49 and Caledonian 0–6–0 No 828.

RIGHT: The fifth LNER Pacific in private ownership is Class A4 Pacific No 60009 *Union of South Africa* which runs on the Lochty Private Railway, a specially-built mile-long line. [W. S. Sellar]

younger. Others include a 3ft gauge Barclay of 1899, *Fair Maid of Foyers*, an electric locomotive and a diesel. The rolling stock collection is worth seeing, too, with a restored Caledonian brake composite of 1921, the Great North of Scotland Railway royal saloon of 1898, a six-wheeled Highland Railway coupe coach of 1908 and a passenger brake of the 1880s, with a similar Glasgow & South Western Railway brake of 1901. Goods stock has not been neglected and apart from Caledonian and GNSR items there is a particularly fine collection of Scottish private owner wagons.

Apart from the large relics, the Scottish RPS also has a small relics museum housed in the former booking office and waiting room at Murrayfield station, Edinburgh. This is open to the public on Saturdays and Sundays from mid-May to mid-September. Also in Edinburgh at the Royal Scottish Museum is one of the earliest steam locomotives, William Hedley's *Wylam Dilly* of 1813. As soon as a new extension has been completed this veteran will be joined by the LNER 4–4–0 *Morayshire*, built at Darlington in 1928 and presented to the Museum by Mr. Ian Fraser of Arbroath. Another engine destined for a museum is the LMS Ivatt 2–6–0 No 46464, built by BR in 1950, and latterly the Carmyllie Pilot, which it is hoped will be housed in a new Dundee Museum.

Glasgow Corporation opened a Transport Museum in 1964 in the former paintshop of the Coplawhill Tramway works. Here were housed some horse drawn and motor vehicles, together with six tramcars. Three years later a railway section was opened and this now houses the Scottish preserved locomotives once so familiar on enthusiast's special trains, thanks to the interest and co-operation of BR Scottish Region. These are the famous Caledonian Railway 4–2–2 No 123 of 1886, which took part in the races to the north between the rival West Coast and East Coast routes in 1888, the Highland Railway " Jones Goods " No 103 of 1894, the first 4–6–0 built for service in this country, North British Railway 4–4–0 No 256 *Glen Douglas* of 1913 and GNSR 4–4–0 No 49 *Gordon Highlander* of 1920. Two other engines have been added to the collection, the last surviving G&SWR engine, 0–6–0T No 9 of 1917, and Caledonian Railway 0–6–0 No 828 of 1899, the latter saved by the Scottish Locomotive Preservation Society. These six engines in the beauty of their old liveries are a sight indeed and can be visited each weekday and on Sunday afternoons.

It is to be hoped that some of the Falkirk engines may steam again even if the others mentioned are no longer likely to do so. But live steam can still be seen North of the Border on the Lochty Private Railway five miles from Anstruther, East Fife. Here Gresley Pacific No 60009 *Union of South Africa*, with one of the " Coronation " beavertail observation cars is steamed on Sunday afternoons between June and August, where it may be seen trundling up and down about a mile of track in a most attractive setting.

Footnote

Throughout the foregoing text mention has been made of the fact that many places may be visited only on open days. The dates of these are usually to be found in RAILWAY WORLD, which also includes subsequent reports and photographs of such events. The Association of Railway Preservation Societies publishes a journal twice each year which gives details of preservation activities and includes addresses of member societies for those wishing to join. This journal, RAILWAY FORUM, is obtainable from the ARPS, 31 Old Croft Road, Walton-on-the-Hill, Stafford, from which address can also be purchased the ARPS Stock Lists describing all preserved steam locomotives and rolling stock in this country. Also dealing with preserved locomotives in more detail, and extensively illustrated is the book *Preserved Locomotives* by H. C. Casserley, published by Ian Allan, available from the publisher or from bookshops.